The Mill
on the
Roeliff Jansen Kill

250 Years of American Industrial History

Harold Faber
Editor

Wesley Keeler
Associate Editor

Brian Yorck
Photographer

David Dwy
Business Manager

Harold Faber, Jeffrey Holmes, Hilary Masters,
Ethel Miller, Sally Naramore Bottiggi,
Peter H. Stott, James Polk
Contributing Authors

Published by

Black Dome Press Corp.
RR1, Box 422
Hensonville, New York 12439
(518)734-6357

In conjunction with

The Roeliff Jansen Historical Society
Box 172
Copake Falls, New York 12517

First Edition, 1993

Library of Congress Card Catalog Number 93-079570

ISBN 0-9628523-9-2

Cover design by Artemisia, Inc.

Printed in the USA

The Roeliff Jansen Historical Society was founded in 1974, in anticipation of the bicentennial of the United States. Its purpose is to discover, collect, preserve, display and disseminate any materials that may help to document or illustrate the history of the Roeliff Jansen area in eastern Columbia County, encompassing the towns of Ancram, Copake, Gallatin, Hillsdale, and Taghkanic. As part of that endeavor, it maintains a historical museum in the hamlet of Copake Falls, New York. The Society was chartered as a non-profit organization by the State Board of Regents in 1975. Its mail address is Box 172, Copake Falls, New York, 12517.

The Society's Museum in the
1892 Copake Falls Methodist Church

Acknowledgements

We would like to thank:

Kenneth Hamm, *The Independent,* Margaret Porter, Ethel Miller, Clara Van Tassel, the Clermont State Historical Site and the United States Military Academy at West Point for permission to use photographs.

Sally Bottiggi Naramore and Peter H. Stott for permission to use their articles in *The Livingston Legacy* and *The History of Industry in Columbia County,* respectively.

Elizabeth Demetriades and her architectural office in Ancramdale for preparing the map of Livingston Manor.

The Columbia County Planning Department for furnishing a map of Columbia County.

The management of the Kimberly-Clark Corporation and the staff of the paper mill in Ancram for their enthusiastic cooperation.

The members of the Roeliff Jansen Historical Society and the staff of Black Dome Press in Hensonville, who made this book possible.

Contents

List of Illustrations

Introduction

by Ethel Miller

Town Historian, Ancram, New York

From the day it was first built 250 years ago, the mill on the Roeliff Jansen Kill has been the center of Ancram. It was built there to take advantage of a 30-foot drop in the kill, which furnished water power for years, first for the iron mill and then for the paper mill that succeeded it.

As you will see in the following pages, the mill was built in 1743 by Philip Livingston, son of the first Lord of Livingston Manor. It was the first and for many years the only ironworks in New York State, operated by Livingston and his son Robert, who did not live in Ancram but in a manor house on the banks of the Hudson River, about fifteen miles away.

When it was operating at full force with several forges, the mill provided employment for between 60 and 100 men as colliers, founders, blacksmiths, and teamsters. At first, the iron ore came from Salisbury, Connecticut, and later from nearby ore beds on the Livingston Manor. It was hauled in large bin-type wagons by teams of oxen to be made into pig iron in furnaces at the mill. After that, the pig iron was forged into iron bars and rods.

During the Revolutionary War, iron from Ancram (and other places, of course) was used in the defense of the rebelling colonies. Some of the iron forged at Ancram was made into huge links fabricated into the chain placed across the Hudson River between Anthony's Nose and Fort Montgomery to keep the British fleet from sailing up the Hudson River.

The first residents of Ancram were farmers brought there in 1740-41 when Livingston settled several families from Scotland (the ancestral home of the Livingston family) on land in the vicinity of Punch Brook and Ancram. The majority of the farmers grew crops, principally wheat, on leased land. Part of the crop was paid as rent to the Lord of the Manor.

But the mill workers came soon after. Although some farm families provided workers for the mill, most of them came in response to advertisements for skilled help placed in New York City newspapers.

In those early days, Ancram was the center of two industries. One was the mill, which produced cast-iron products such as stoves, grates, firebacks, pots and kettles, shot and cannon balls and pig iron for nearby forges. The other was farming.

The farmers raised so many sheep that Ancram became one of the leading sheep-producing areas of New York State. Later, Ancram's farmers converted to dairy cows, and black and white Holstein cows became a familiar sight in the pastures of the town (and still are, although dairy farming is a declining industry in Ancram and New York generally).

Since the opening of the mill, many changes have taken place in both Ancram and its mill. The iron mill came upon hard times and was sold at a foreclosure sale in 1845, just about the time the anti-rent wars resulted in an end to the manorial system of land tenure in Ancram and the rest of the state.

In 1854, the remnants of the old mill were torn down. A paper mill, employing 62 men, was erected on the property. Through times of frequent financial trouble, that paper mill, rebuilt and expanded several times, has remained in operation. It is one of the largest employers in Columbia County.

The mill was (and is today) the principal source of employment and revenue for the full-time residents of Ancram. By 1830, Ancram's population had risen to 1,533, just about what it is today. But today's population mix has changed dramatically, from farm families and workers of the mill's early years to a more mixed group of farmers, local residents, second-home owners—and mill workers. In a changing community, one thing has remained a constant—the mill on the falls of the Roeliff Jansen Kill in Ancram, a source of pride not only for the men and women who work there, but for the entire region as well.

A Chronology of the Mill
on the Roeliff Jansen Kill

1743	Original mill opened as an iron forge, the first in the colony of New York.
1776	The mill furnishes iron bars for the American Revolutionary Army; chain links for Hudson River barrier.
1804	Ancram Turnpike Company organized to improve road between Salisbury and the Hudson River.
1814	The Town of Ancram is organized.
1830	The Town of Gallatin is created out of the west end of Ancram.
1845	The iron mill ceases operations.
1852	The New York & Harlem Railroad links Ancram to New York City.
1853	Elizur Smith and George Platner organize the Ancram Paper Company and acquire the old Livingston property.
1854	The mill is completely rebuilt; begins operations as a paper mill, using rags and straw, employing 62 men.
1860	The Peaslees purchase the mill.
1885	The mill fails, following the death of Horace Peaslee.
1889	Sigmund D. Rosenbaum takes over ownership of the mill and begins manufacture of straw wrapping paper.
1905	The Ancram Paper Mill is incorporated.
1908	Parts of the mill rebuilt after a fire.
1921	The Standard Products Company buys the mill and begins making carbon and lightweight tissue paper.
1927	The mill is completely electrified.
1953	The mill is closed.
1954	A Citizens' Committee formed to save the mill.
1955	The Peter J. Schweitzer Company buys the mill and begins production of reconstituted tobacco products.
1957	The Kimberly-Clark Corporation purchases the Schweitzer Company and the mill.
1989-'91	The paper-making machines are computerized.
1993	The mill celebrates its 250th birthday.

1

The Livingston Iron Mill

By Sally Bottiggi Naramore

Soon after the English settlement of North America began, colonists started the search for a means to produce iron. The new settlers required necessities such as kettles, wagon boxes, hoes, axe heads, and firebacks—items whose weight made them difficult to import from the mother country. In return the English anxiously sought to import new sources of iron ore. As early as 1608, Virginia colonists responded to this need by sending iron ore to England.[1]

The transformation of the readily available bog iron into usable products garnered the interest of the colonists more than simply shipping the raw material to English forges. Bog iron was found in abundance in stream beds and near the earth's surface. Massachusetts settlers established North America's first ironworks at Saugus, where an iron furnace and forge were built in 1643. This ironworks relied upon the bog iron found in the Saugus River. Soon other blast furnaces emerged on the New England countryside near streams supplying both iron ore and the power for the works.[2] Several furnaces also emerged in New Jersey where Colonel Lewis Morris built a furnace and forge near Tinton Falls in Monmouth County.[3]

In spite of this development, these early ironworks produced minimally and created little impact on the worldwide industry. By the mid-eighteenth century, however, the colonies experienced a substantial rise in the construction of ironworks, and by 1775 colonial iron production ranked ahead of England, making the colonies an integral part of the worldwide market.[4] During the 1730s, the North American iron industry expanded at a particularly rapid rate for three main reasons: increased settlement, population growth, and rise in market demand.[5] Two colonies, New Jersey and Pennsylvania, led in this development.

In New Jersey, new ironworks developed near the first forge built by Lewis Morris in the seventeenth century. These ironworks in northern New Jersey had the advantage of being near waterpower and iron ore deposits in the Ramapo Mountains.[6] The same two conditions occurred in the hinterland of Pennsylvania along the Schuykill, Delaware, Lehigh, and Susquehanna rivers.[7] Also, the growing shipbuilding industry in Philadelphia added another incentive to the ironmasters in Pennsylvania.

As an active merchant, Philip Livingston, second lord of Livingston Manor, was well aware of the worldwide economy and sought ways of profiting from it. He realized the growing need for iron in the colonies and its profit potential in the overseas market. He first expressed interest in iron production when he purchased land in Connecticut with two New Englanders—his distant cousin, Jacob Wendell, and John Stoddard.

The three men acquired land just east of the Taconic Hills and Livingston Manor, near Salisbury, where Livingston learned that iron ore had been discovered in 1731. He desired to build an ironworks on their new land,[8] but eventual disagreements among the partners about land use and tenant farmers caused Philip to sell his share of the property. The New Englanders wanted to sell the land in parcels while Livingston preferred leasing the land to Dutch and English farmers.[9]

Despite this setback, he continued to pursue his quest for an ironworks. Even before he sold his land in Connecticut, he formulated plans for an iron furnace and forge at a site just west of the Taconic Hills on the Roeliff Jansen Creek in the southeastern part of Livingston Manor, an area called Ancram after his father's Scottish birthplace.

Philip's decision to place his ironworks on the manor greatly influenced the growth and success of the Ancram ironworks. Elements of the manorial system such as the availability of tenant labor, as well as shipping interests and mercantile experience, helped make the Ancram iron furnace and forge a profitable and useful venture for the Livingston family from 1743 to 1790. The manor gave Philip, and later his son Robert, an advantage over their other ironmaking competitors in New England, New Jersey, and Pennsylvania.

To understand fully the benefits the manor provided the Livingstons, we must examine the technical aspects of iron production and marketing. All colonial ironmakers had to surmount the same basic problems in order to insure a profitable business: production, transportation, and marketing. Each of these components posed special difficulties.

The most complex and important element was production. Far from being an exact science, iron production in the eighteenth century relied upon the careful orchestration of raw materials. Only skilled, experienced men working with superior raw materials could create a quality iron. Philip Livingston expressed this fact in a letter to his son Robert: "The profits in iron works if the ore be good, the works well made and skilled workmen is the most considerable than anything I ever heard of but if one of these three fails all signify nothing."[10]

Three raw materials produced iron: iron ore, limestone, and charcoal. These substances, once heated, created smelted iron. To produce the adequate temperature, a special furnace was necessary. In the eighteenth century, iron producers built furnaces of brick lined with sandstone or slate. These large cone-shaped edifices rose upwards of 22-35 feet high.[11] Ironmakers combined the three ingredients and then fired the pile.

Attached to the bottom of the furnace was a bellows powered by a trip hammer connected to a water wheel. As the bellows moved up and down, it forced air into the bottom of the furnace through a nozzle called the tuyere.[12] Once the fire began and the bellows started, ironmasters announced that their furnace had begun to blast.[13] Blasts usually occurred from October through December, and April through July or August.[14]

Once the blast, which took several weeks, finished, founders tapped the furnace from the crucible at the bottom. The molten iron poured out of the crucible into channels of sand on the floor. These channels had the appearance of a sow suckling her piglets; consequently, ironworkers called it "pig iron" or "pig metal."[15] Founders also molded the sand into specific shapes for items such as kettles, pots, and firebacks. All the impurities of the iron floated to the top as slag and were poured out after the iron; workmen simply discarded the slag.[16]

Ironmasters sold the pig iron or sent it to their forge to be formed into bar iron. Most iron furnaces had a forge or finery as part of the ironworks. The Ancram ironworks included two forges with bellows. Alexander Coventry, an English traveler, described the works in his diary:

> *There are two forges in the uppermost building.*
> *These are built in the form of large ovens, seem-*
> *ingly about 10 feet wide and 6 feet high, and*
> *each has two enormous, large bellows. The*
> *muzzles, or pipes of which discharge into this*
> *cavity. This is for refining the ore after being*
> *melted in the furnace.[17]*

Forgemen or finers placed the pig metal in a fire and then pounded it with a trip hammer powered by a water wheel. Finers shaped the pig into long, thin, barbell-shaped items called anconies. The anconies were sold or taken to the chafery. At the chafery, another type of forge, workmen pounded the heated anconies into bars.[18] Blacksmiths used bar iron, a purer iron than pig, to forge utensils, tools, or other items. This specialized iron received a high market price.[19]

Of the three raw materials necessary to produce pig iron, two, iron ore and limestone, needed no special processing. Eighteenth-century ironmakers speak very little of the quality of the limestone, but they do of the iron ore. Philip Livingston used ore from Salisbury, Connecticut, and later in the 1770s, his son Robert used ore mined on the manor property. Both sources were of high quality, helping to insure a valuable finished product.

The weight of iron ore made transporting it difficult and expensive. Consequently, the iron manufacturers in Pennsylvania and New Jersey placed their works near their source of the ore, as did Philip Livingston. By building their ironworks near ore deposits, ironmasters in the mid-Atlantic colonies were forced to place their works far from major population centers.

Of all the raw material, charcoal created the most difficulty in manufacture. Semi-skilled laborers called colliers made the charcoal by firing wood in a dome made of sticks and clay. The burning occurred during the dry season, usually in late spring and early fall. Colliers had to be careful to use the correct size sticks in order to produce proper charcoal.[20] Philip Livingston, in his agreement with Ebenezer Loomis to coal 2,000 cords of wood, stated specifically that there be no "branches" in the charcoal for the furnaces and "no branches longer than six inches" in the charcoal for the forge.[21] Sources on charcoal making, although specific about the size of the sticks, do not mention the type of wood preferred.

The activities of all ironworks, including Ancram, revolved around the production of charcoal. Without charcoal neither the furnace not the forge could operate. The availability of charcoal set the rhythm for the whole works.[22] Both Robert and his father wrote in their letters of the problem of running out of charcoal.[23]

To transform these raw materials into iron required not only a reliable pool of labor, but also a large capital outlay. In addition to the cost of building the furnace and forge, iron producers built roads and bridges, workers' housing, saw or grist mills, and dams to divert the water to their works. In 1766 Peter Hasenclever, a prominent iron producer and entrepreneur from Germany who settled in New Jersey, described his latest ironworks. Hasenclever's works at Long Pond contained twenty-three buildings: a forge with four fires, a furnace, two coal-houses, six log-houses, a storehouse, six collier houses, a sawmill, a horse stable, a reservoir, two ponds, and two bridges.[24]

Philip Livingston became staggeringly aware of the capital costs very early in his venture. He mentioned in a letter to Jacob Wendell in 1741 that he anticipated a capital outlay of £6,000.[25] He also felt that it would be a long time before the investment was realized. In a letter to his son Robert on January 30, 1745, two years after the works' first blast, he noted with optimism:

> *Iron Manufactory is the most advantagious business if well managed and carryed on with honest and skillful hands that we have in America and am fully convinced that ours will answer exceeding well but will cost a Vast sum of Money before it be completed and will take a Considerable time before all Expenses be paid.*[26]

Despite his concerns, Livingston had the advantage over his competitors. His vast fortune allowed him to expend large sums without taking on partners. Peter Hasenclever, at his works in Ringwood, New Jersey and Sterling, New York, as well as the major producers in Pennsylvania, sold shares in their works in order to start and continue operations.[27] Philip and Robert Livingston had the unique opportunity among colonial ironmakers to solely own their works.

Another difficulty in iron production was labor. As the description of iron technology suggests, the work was labor-intensive. Iron production required three types of workers: skilled, semi-skilled, and unskilled. The unskilled workers formed the largest group and included wood-cutters, carters, and laborers. Ironworks owners found it difficult to hire seasonal laborers because the ironworks were located in underpopulated areas. Wood-cutters, for example, primarily worked the month or two before the charcoal pits were fired. Ironmasters needed to secure many laborers for a short duration of time in essentially uninhabited areas.[28]

In Pennsylvania, many ironworks owners tried to use slave labor or indentured servants for such work, a group that frequently had a tendency to run away.[29] The Livingstons, although faced with the same problem, once again benefited from the resources of the manor. They could call on tenant farmers to cart ore or chop wood for the furnaces as part of their yearly obligations under the terms of their leases.[30] Semi-skilled laborers such as colliers, wheelwrights, masons, and blacksmiths found employment at the ironworks throughout the colonies. Colliers, in particular, were in constant demand. Philip Livingston expressed their importance in his agreement with Ebenezer Loomis, who was to coal for him. The document contained a passage that bound both parties to complete their agreement; if either one failed to complete the terms of the agreement, he had to pay a £200 bond to the other. This stipulation illustrates not only how important a collier's work was to Livingston, but that Loomis had the ability to demand the same assurance from Livingston.[31]

Of all the types of laborers, skilled workers such as finers, chafers, hammermen, and founders demanded the highest wages because they were in shortest supply. Since the colonial iron industry was just developing, few Americans knew the trade. This labor shortage compelled iron producers to seek out Europeans, especially English and German laborers.

Importing workers added to the already high costs of maintaining an iron furnace and forge. Philip Livingston illustrated the hold these men had on production in a letter to Jacob Wendell. Wendell asked for a shipment of bar iron of specific size, 3/4" square. The refiners at Ancram simply refused to produce such iron and stated that it was too difficult to make.[32] In the final stages of ironmaking, the ironworks owner relied entirely on his skilled laborers for a quality product. In this area, the Livingstons had no more advantage than their fellow ironmasters.

Ironmasters combatted the high wages the skilled and semi-skilled laborers demanded by paying their workers at the end of a production cycle. This method kept down the amount of cash paid to workers, since during the working cycle laborers charged necessities to the company store. Consequently, at the end of the working season the owner owed little if any money to the workers. The company store provided the only means of acquiring items since the works were located so far from any towns. The Livingstons managed their operations in the same manner. They made a profit since they purchased sundries and other necessities for their other stores in New York, Albany, and Schenectady. Also, their tenant farmers brought their wheat owed for rent occasionally to Ancram to supply the store. All of this helped defer the need to use scarce currency before the iron reached the market.[33]

The location of ironworks in colonial America convenient to the iron ore and water power nonetheless created a problem. By placing the ironworks near the ore, the ironmasters inadvertently created a transportation problem. These ironworks were rarely connected with population centers by usable roads or waterways. Iron manufacturers had to find ways of moving supplies cheaply to the site and the product to market if they were to be competitive. In both cases, overland travel was the only means of moving the necessary cargo for most colonial ironmasters.

In Pennsylvania, rivers near the ironworks such as the Lehigh and Susquehanna flowed over rough rocky areas that made boat transport impossible.[34] Furthermore, the Pennsylvania township authorities where the ironworks were located often refused to build the necessary roads.[35] The combination of poor conditions and the need to hire carters created yet another expensive obstacle for iron producers.

In this aspect of the iron business, the Livingstons possessed a true advantage. Although they did have to transport supplies and the finished product overland to the Hudson, some fifteen miles away, they owned the land over which the goods traversed. Consequently, if they chose to build a road from the manor wharf to Ancram, they had the authority to do so. Tenant farmers on the manor were required to maintain the roads at the bidding of the manor lord according to their lease agreement.[36] Furthermore, tenants frequently gave two or more days of hauling to fulfill their agreement.[37]

After the finished product reached a town, the ironworks owner faced other complications. He had to deliver goods to a major market or else be content to sell his wares at the local market to blacksmiths and forgemen. In Pennsylvania, the best market existed in Philadelphia. As mentioned, the only means of transportation was by wagon.

By 1767 a stage coach known as the "Flying Machine" had cut travel time from the Hopewell iron forge to Philadelphia to two days; however, this vehicle carried passengers, not heavy pig and bar iron.[38] In addition to the time factor, land travel cost far more than water transportation.[39] Even in New Jersey, where the finished product would travel to New York City by water, the ironmasters still had to arrange land transport to waterways; and once there, they had to pay for ferry or boat service to haul the cargo to New York City.

The Livingstons not only had an easier means of overland travel but had advantages in water transportation as well. Both Philip and Robert Livingston were shipowners, and had access to additional shipping through partnerships with other family members.[40] Their ownership of ships that made frequent trips up the Hudson River created an easy and economical means of transporting their finished product to the major market in New York. These vessels also carried iron to markets in Boston and England.[41] These accessible methods of transportation relieved the Livingstons of one more major expense in the production of iron and allowed them to profit more from the market price.

Even if an ironmaster succeeded in producing quality iron and getting it to market, he realized no profit until the iron sold. The location of the ironworks in the hinterland not only made transportation difficult, but also made sales complicated.

An individual owning an iron furnace without partners had two choices in marketing his product. He could sell his iron in the local market, which was limited and usually less profitable, or he could sell on the colonial and international markets. In order to accomplish the second means of sale, the ironmaster often had to sell shares in his corporation to merchants. These partners provided credit and overseas contacts as well as the expertise to control a commodities market. This marketing technique gave the ironworks owner higher profits but at the cost of decentralized and often uncoordinated organization. The conflict arose from the shareholders making decisions by committee. As a result, the ironworks owner lost control of his sales operation.[42] As in the other aspects of the iron business, the Livingstons again had an advantage over their competitors. Livingston Manor, from its earliest beginnings under the first lord, had been heavily involved in the mercantile trade.

By the time Philip Livingston opened his first ironworks at Ancram, an established system of sending raw materials from the manor to market existed. Both Philip and the third lord, Robert, received training in the merchant field before they inherited the manor. Their siblings of both generations were also trained as merchants and served as agents for the manor lords. Philip Livingston, for example, traded with his brothers Robert, Jr. and Gilbert, and used his son Robert as his agent in New York. Like his father, the third lord used his sons as agents and traded with his cousins in Barbados and Dutchess County.

Both father and son were fortunate to have their cousin, Jacob Wendell, represent them in the Boston and London markets. This mercantile system involved members of the family and thus kept profits and control of sales within a select group of relatives. Furthermore, the expertise both Philip and Robert acquired in the commodities market made them aware of the risks involved with the international market.

In order to find buyers for their product, iron producers needed agents to represent them in port cities such as New York, Philadelphia, and Boston. For individual owners in the local market this was not a concern, although for the larger partnerships it was. Often a merchant partner in these larger multi-owner businesses accepted the responsibility of representing the business. Otherwise, the group had to pay someone.[44] Again, the Livingstons escaped this worry. Both manor lords relied on their sons to represent them in the New York City market and to find English buyers. In Boston, another relative, Jacob Wendell, acted as their agent.

Trustworthy and able merchants at the marketplace helped the Livingstons prosper in the decidedly flexible and complex iron market. Letters between Philip Livingston and his son or Jacob Wendell showed how important communication was to the success of the operation. Robert, Jr. constantly kept his father abreast of the market price per ton of iron during the first six years of the ironworks. The average price at the time was £9, New York currency, per ton of pig iron. Philip preferred to sell his iron for cash rather than trade it for other merchandise. He also avoided currency other than New York's. However, in one letter to Jacob Wendell he did consent to take New England money.[45] Such communication enabled him to make informed decisions on the sales of his product.

Robert Livingston used the same technique as his father to market his iron. He conferred with his sons Peter R. and Philip, and later with Walter, Robert Cambridge, and Henry, who all acted as his New York agents. Jacob Wendell continued to look after the Livingstons' interest in Boston. Robert took the same keen interest as his father in the price of the iron. In a letter to Jacob Wendell dated March 12, 1755, Robert stated that he would sell his iron for £9 per ton.[46] Like his father, Robert preferred cash, although he did accept payment in kind and allowed certain buyers to build accounts to be paid at a later date. In a letter to Robert Livingston, his son Walter explained how he would exchange twenty tons of pig iron to a Rhode Island merchant for West Indies and New England rum. He went on to say, however, that he hoped that the balance owed him would be paid for in cash in the spring.[47]

As the letter from Walter suggests, despite their wishes, ironworks owners often had to be content to trade their iron for other products. The manor's place in international trade allowed the manor lords to accept and make good use of other commodities such as rum, molasses, and sundry goods from England, which were traded at a profit along with wheat and flour from the manor.[48] Advertisements in the New York *Mercury*, a merchants' newspaper of the mid-eighteenth century, attest to the number of items sold in the Livingstons' store and the frequency with which their ships left for Europe and the West Indies.[49]

The close relationship between the agents and the Livingstons provided the manor lords with an up-to-date knowledge of the market demand. For instance, Philip Livingston asked Wendell in one letter to advise him on the type of iron, bar or pig, that was most in demand.[50] In a letter from an agent, James Elliot, to Robert Livingston, the former recommended that "casting makes a better market than Piggs, provided we can make them as good and cheap as other people. I question not but the Country Merchants will take Quantities allowing that they may retail with Reasonable Profits."[51]

Although other ironmakers may have had the same advice from their agents, they would not have had the intimacy of a family relationship. Evidence also suggests a lack of harmony among the large group-owned ironworks that competed with the Livingstons' works.[52] In any case, the mercantile system worked to the Livingston family's advantage in iron as it did in other commodities. In 1769, Walter and Robert Cambridge Livingston credited their father's accounts at £10,092, and most of the money came from the sale of iron.

In 1739, Philip Livingston expressed a dream to build an ironworks that would rival those of the other colonies. He and his son Robert fulfilled that aspiration by constructing three ironworks in all, the one at Ancram being the largest. Their success in great measure was due to the benefits derived from the manorial system. They had ready supplies of raw materials, unskilled manpower, transportation networks, and a trading empire. These advantages gave them more chance for profit and less chance for failure. Unlike the sole owner of a Pennsylvania ironworks or even an entrepreneur like Peter Hasenclever, the Livingstons survived on more than just the profits from the ironworks. The ironworks, like tenant farms, ships, and stores were just a part of the larger manorial system.

Reprinted from *The Livingston Legacy*, a publication of Bard College/Hudson Valley Studies Program, 1987.

How Big Was the Livingston Manor?

The original manor stretched from east to west about twenty miles, from the Hudson River to the Massachusetts and Connecticut borders, and north to south about twelve miles, a total of 160,240 acres. It included the present-day towns of Livingston, Germantown, Clermont, Taghkanic, Gallatin, Copake, and Ancram.

Notes

1. Arthur C. Binning, *Pennsylvania Iron Manufacture in the Eighteenth Century* (Harrisburg: Pennsylvania Historical Commission, 1938), p. 14.
2. Ibid., p. 16.
3. Ibid., p. 20.
4. Arthur C. Binning, *British Regulation of the Colonial Iron Industry* (Philadelphia: University of Pennsylvania Press, 1933), p. 4.
5. Binning, *Pennsylvania Iron*, p. 82.
6. James M. Ransom, *Vanishing Ironworks of the Ramapos: The Story of Forges, Furnaces and Mines of the New Jersey-New York Border Area* (New Brunswick: Rutgers University Press, 1966), p. 3.
7. Paul F. Paskoff, *Industrial Revolution: Organization, Structure and Growth of the Pennsylvania Iron Industry, 1750-1860* (Baltimore and London: The Johns Hopkins University Press, 1983), p. 51.
8. Joan Gordon, "The Livingstons of New York 1675-1860: Kinship and Class," Diss. Columbia University 1959, p. 92.
9. Ibid., p. 89.
10. Philip Livingston to his son Robert, May 12, 1742, Livingston-Redmond Papers, Roosevelt Library.
11. Ransom, pp.7-8.
12. Paskoff, p. 7.
13. Ransom, p. 11.
14. Paskoff, p. 19.
15. Ibid., p. 7.
16. Ransom, p. 10.
17. Journal of Alexander Coventry, Wednesday, April 17, 1790, p. 407.
18. Paskoff, p. 8.
19. In a letter dated August 14, 1776, Robert Livingston, Jr., quoted Philip Van Rensselaer a price of £40 per ton. On February of that same year Walter Livingston, son of Robert, quoted his father a price of £30 per ton. Robert Livingston to Philip Van Rensselaer, August 14, 1776, Livingston Papers, New York State Archives. Walter Livingston to Robert Livingston, Jr., February 18, 1776, Livingston-Redmond Papers, Roosevelt Library.
20. Paskoff, p. 18.
21. Agreement between Ebenezer Loomis and Philip Livingston, April 14, 1748, Livingston-Redmond Papers, Roosevelt Library.
22. Paskoff, p. 18.
23. Philip Livingston to his son Robert, May 12, 1742, Livingston-Redmond Papers. James Elliot to Robert Livingston, April 16, 1766, Livingston-Redmond Papers. Robert Livingston to Jacob Wendell, March 12, 1755, Livingston Papers, Museum of the City of New York.
24. Ransom, p. 78. Philip Livingston built a saw and a grist mill as part of his Ancram works.

25. Philip Livingston to Jacob Wendell, March 25, 1741, Livingston Papers, Museum of the City of New York.

26. Philip Livingston to his son Robert, January 30, 1745, Livingston-Redmond Papers.

27. Durham Iron Works in Pennsylvania is an example of a complex, multi-owner ironworks. Paskoff, p. 3. Peter Hasenclever had several partners who invested in his Ringwood, New Jersey works and at his works at Sterling, New York. Bining, *Pennsylvania Iron,* p. 18, and see Ransom, p. 22.

28. Paskoff, p. 8.

29. Ibid., p. 15.

30. In Robert Livingston, Jr.'s Rent book for the years 1767-1782, nearly every tenant gave labor or carted materials to or from Ancram at least once during that period. Some gave such service on a yearly basis. See Robert Livingston's Rent List, Robert R. Livingston Papers, Series VI.

31. Agreement between Ebenezer Loomis and Philip Livingston, April 14, 1748, Livingston-Redmond Papers.

32. Philip Livingston to Jacob Wendell, April 5, 1746, Livingston Papers, Museum of the City of New York.

33. Robert Livingston, Jr., to his son Robert Cambridge, September 8, 1766, Livingston-Redmond Papers.

34. Paskoff, p. 8.

35. Ibid., p. 9.

36. Gordon, p. 77.

37. Robert Livingston's Rent List, Robert R. Livingston Papers, Series VI.

38. Paskoff, p. 40

39. George Rodgers Taylor, *The Transportation Revolution, 1815-1860* (Armonk: M. E. Sharpe, Inc., 1951), p. 135.

40. Gordon, p. 97. Philip Livingston owned eight ships between 1726 and 1749, in some of which he shared ownership with family members. Gordon, p. 124. Robert Livingston, Jr., owned four ships in partnership with his father and two solely—the *Ancram* and the *Prince Charles.*

41. Gordon, p. 139.

42. Paskoff, p. 3. A good example of a multi-owner and international iron-works is the Durham Iron Works of Pennsylvania. Also, Peter Hasenclever and other New Jersey ironworks owners sold shares of their operations to offset expenses and to participate in a larger marketplace.

43. Gordon, pp. 2, 56. For more information on the mercantile and business elements of the manor system in New York, see Sung Bok Kim, *Landlord and Tenant in Colonial New York Manorial Society, 1664-1775* (Chapel Hill: University of North Carolina Press, 1978).

44. Paskoff, p. 3.

45. Philip Livingston to Jacob Wendell, September 4, 1744, Livingston Papers, Museum of the City of New York.

46. Robert Livingston, Jr., to Jacob Wendell, March 12, 1775, Livingston Papers, Museum of the City of New York.

47. Robert Livingston, Jr., to his son Walter, December 24, 1766, Livingston-Redmond Papers.

48. Gordon, p. 96.

49. The following advertisements of Robert and Philip Livingston's ships setting sail are just a sampling of those listed in the New York *Mercury* for the years 1752-1766:

    August 3, 1752—the ship *Nebuchadnezar* for London;

    November 6, 1752—the sailing of the ship *Snow* for London;

    April 10, 1758—the sailing of the ship *The Charles* to London. There are also advertisements during the same period describing goods available for sale at the Livingston store in New York City. The goods usually consisted of sugar, molasses, household items, spices, pewter, and various sundries. But the advertisements never list pig or bar iron or cast items. One advertisement did list nails. A sample of the advertisements follows:

    February 6, 1752; February 10, 1755; April 6, 1758;

    August 11, 1760; July 18, 1763; and February 24, 1766.

50. Philip Livingston to Jacob Wendell, June 17, 1746, Livingston Papers, Museum of the City of New York.

51. James Elliot to Robert Livingston, Jr., April 16, 1766, Livingston-Redmond Papers.

52. Paskoff, p. 3. Ransom p. 22.

The Founder of Livingston Manor

The founder of the Livingston family in America was Robert Livingston (1664-1728). A talented and ambitious Scotsman, he had been raised in the Netherlands, where his father, a leader in the Scottish church, had taken the family into exile in 1663 after fighting with King Charles II of England.

After his father's death, Livingston came to America at the age of 20. He arrived in Albany, determined to make a fortune in the lucrative fur trade. Fluent in both English and Dutch, Livingston ingratiated himself with both the old Dutch families and their new English masters.

With a good knowledge of international trade, he soon became clerk of the Albany General court, tax collector, secretary to the colony's board of Indian Commissioners, and clerk of the county's greatest private landholders, the Van Rensselaers. His entry into the aristocracy of colonial New York was assured when in 1679, at the age of 25, he married the widow of his former employer on the Patroonship of Rensselaerswyck, Alida Schuyler Van Rensselaer.

On July 22, 1686, he acquired the manor of Livingston, granted by Governor Thomas Dongan. It covered 160,240 acres on the east bank of the Hudson River, about forty miles south of Albany. It became the base of the Livingston family and fortune.

2

The Chain Across the Hudson River

By Harold Faber

Although Ancram itself was isolated from the battles of the American Revolutionary War, the mill on the Roeliff Jansen Kill became a major forge for the Continental Army. One of its little-known but important contributions was to furnish iron for a chain spread across the Hudson River to prevent the British fleet from sailing up the river and thus cutting the thirteen colonies in two.

First, we should mention that two chains were constructed across the Hudson River during the war. The first chain, between Fort Montgomery and Anthony's Nose, just north of the present Bear Mountain Bridge, was built in 1777. The second chain, between West Point and Constitution Island, was built in 1778.

The Ancram ironworks furnished materials for the first chain. The ironworks was operated by Colonel Robert Livingston, Jr., the eldest son of Philip Livingston, the man who founded it. (He is sometimes confused with his cousin, the well-known Robert R. Livingston, who was a member of the governing body of New York State and who later became the chancellor, or chief judge of New York. Robert R. Livingston administered the oath of office to George Washington in 1789 as the first president of the United States and in 1803 became the key figure in the purchase of Louisiana from France.) Colonel Robert Livingston supervised the Ancram enterprise from his manor house on the Hudson River, relying on clerks and managers on the scene.

From the beginning of the war in 1775, Colonel Livingston put the ironworks at the disposal of the state. It turned out two types of products: castings, such as cannonballs, shot, and even possibly small cannons, and bar iron sent to Albany where blacksmiths worked the bars into axes, spades, shovels, and bolts.

A year later, the bar iron took on greater importance. Early in the war, the Continental Congress, sitting in Philadelphia, recognized the strategic importance of the Hudson River. It appointed a committee "to discover where it will be more advisable and proper to obstruct the navigation."

The recommendation soon came back: build a major fort on the river at one of its narrow points and block the river "by means of four or five Booms chained together on one Side of the River, ready to be drawn across" so that "the Passage can be closed to prevent any Vessel from passing or repassing."

Two forts were built in the mid-Hudson where the channel decreases to a width of about 1,500 feet: Fort Constitution, opposite the present-day West Point, and Fort Montgomery, named after General Richard Montgomery, who had been killed in 1775 at the Battle of Quebec, on a hill immediately to the north of the present Bear Mountain Bridge.

Immediately, New York's governing body began to make plans to obstruct the Hudson as well. It adopted a resolution, which stated:

> *"That in order to prevent any of the Ships of the King of Great Britain coming up Hudson's River, it will be necessary to throw across the River at or near Fort Montgomery a Boom of Pine Logs not less than 50 feet long, placed ten feet apart,*

*and framed together by three cross Pieces; that
each Raft be placed 15 feet apart and Connected
by strong Chains of 1 1/2 inch iron; that the
Rafts be anchored with their Butts down the
River; and the Butts be armored with Iron."*

It was soon learned that a supply of 50-foot logs
was not available on the Hudson south of Albany. So the
plans were revised—to install a chain of heavy iron links
across the river at Fort Montgomery.

Already the kind of iron needed to forge the chain
links had been ordered for a different purpose—to build a
similar chain across the Richelieu River in northern New
York to prevent British ships from Canada from sailing into
Lake Champlain. The bar iron was ordered from two
sources, Mount Hope in northern New Jersey and from
Ancram.

When the Richelieu project was abandoned, the Fort
Montgomery plan grew in importance. Ancram was ordered to continue smelting and manufacturing bar iron
about 1 1/2 inches square to be sent to Poughkeepsie. The
order contained these numbers—600 yards or 1,800 feet of
chain, to be made from 4,800 feet of bar iron in length.

Iron ore for the Ancram smelter came from local
beds and from Salisbury. After the ore was melted, the
blast furnace at Ancram cast pig iron, which was hammered
into anconies or dumbbell-shaped iron bars with large
square ends. The ends helped blacksmiths maneuver the
anconies into place under the hammers. After the iron between the ends was hammered to a 1 1/2 inch square
thickness and several feet long, the ends were cut off.

From the ironworks at Ancram, the finished bars
were carted by wagons to the Livingston wharf on the
Hudson River. On August 11, 1776, Livingston requested
that a ship be sent up the river to pick up the bars. He wrote:

*"I have now brought down to my Wharf two tuns
of Iron, and there is now three tuns more drawn,
ready to come down on Tuesday; and expect
Saturday to have five tuns more. All the Iron
made since your last orders is 2 inch, and the
bars as long as we could make them."*

The ship's captain reported loading 185 iron bars.
Livingston claimed he sent 205. They went to Poughkeepsie's Kemble forge where foundry workers and blacksmiths heated the bars to a cherry red color, hammered
them, and shaped them into links for the chain. Each link
was about 14 inches long and weighed about 40 to 50
pounds. But there was a dispute about the price. Although
Livingston had charged civilian customers about 20
pounds, then still the British unit of currency in America,
for a ton, he told the state that the bar iron would now cost
more then twice as much, 45 pounds a ton.

The reason, he said, was inflation that affected his
workmen at the Ancram mill. He gave this explanation,
"my Workmen cannot work at the same wages they have
done, every Article they want to support their Famileys
being double, and some Articles, such as linens, being more
than double."

He had another reason as well. An unusual summer
drought made it necessary for him to dig a new feeder
sluice on the Roeliff Jansen Kill to maintain the level of the
pond near the mill, which he used to furnish water power
for his triphammers.

Not only was there an argument about how many
iron bars were sent and the price, but Livingston was worried about being paid. In September, he sent New York a
bill for 902 pounds for the iron shipped by that date.

He was right to be worried. Almost by return mail,
he received a letter from the state treasurer that said, "We
are sorry that after inspecting our Treasury, we find our

Finances so low that we cannot possibly pay you the full sum on the Iron that has been received." Livingston promptly slowed down his shipments of iron bars.

Somehow the dispute was resolved. And another positive step was taken. Lieutenant Thomas Machin, a 32-year-old engineer, was appointed to take charge of the chain project. He arrived on the scene in October 1776, after recovering from wounds suffered at the Battle of Bunker Hill.

Lieutenant Machin was an energetic young man. He ordered additional iron links to be made at the Ringwood Furnace in northern New Jersey to add to the links made from iron at Ancram. He assembled the chain on log rafts near New Windsor and floated it downriver to Fort Montgomery.

On a cold day in November, the assembled log rafts carrying the chain were drawn across the Hudson and anchored firmly at both ends — at Fort Montgomery and Anthony's Nose. Everyone there knew it was merely a test; the chain would have to be removed for the winter (because it obviously would be damaged by ice in the frozen river), stored, and then reassembled in the spring.

But the chain failed the test. As the tide ran out, the center of the line of log rafts was carried south until it formed a great arc, firmly anchored on both sides of the river. The pressure of the water in the center caused a weak connector to snap and the separated sections of the chain slowly floated south until they came to rest on the shores of the river.

Not discouraged, Machin went back to work after the winter of 1776. By the end of March 1977, his repaired and reinforced chain was placed back into the river, again between Fort Montgomery and Anthony's Nose. It consisted of about 850 chain-links, resting on three-foot wide pine rafts, spanning 1,650 feet, and weighing about 35 tons.

This time it was strong enough to resist the tides. Governor George Clinton wrote to General George Washington on April 18, "As it is now fixed, the tide has not made the least impression on it; it is greatly strengthened by a number of anchors and cables."

And so for a brief time, the iron smelted in Ancram and forged in Poughkeepsie served its wartime purpose of keeping the British fleet at bay—temporarily. The British navy made no attempt to breach the chain by a frontal attack.

Instead, in October 1777, as part of a British plan to cut the colonies in two by a double-pronged attack—south from Canada and north from New York City—the redcoats attacked by land. Under the command of Sir Henry Clinton (no relation to New York's Governor George Clinton), British troops marched north around Bear Mountain and attacked Forts Montgomery and Clinton by land, capturing both.

After the forts were captured, the British fleet sailed north to the chain, cut its links and sailed farther north to capture Fort Constitution across the river from West Point. One of the British naval officers reported: "I have directed such part of the Chain and Boom as cannot be saved to be destroyed; the construction of both give strong Proofs of Labour, Industry and Skill."

The British fleet sailed north, landing at Kingston, then the capital of New York State. They burned it to the ground on October 16. One group of the British invaders sailed farther north, landing at Clermont, the seat of the Livingston family, and burned it to the ground, too.

But the British attempt to divide the colonies failed when General John Burgoyne surrendered the northern army of the two-pronged attack to the Americans at Saratoga. As a result, the southern prong, the one that had reached as far north as Kingston and Clermont, retreated back to New York City.

A year later, in 1778, the second chain across the Hudson River, made without iron from Ancram, was installed between West Point and Fort Constitution. It was never challenged by the British navy or army.

More than fifty years later, in 1830, several links of the great chain between Fort Montgomery and Anthony's Nose were dredged up from the bottom of the river. A newspaper account at the time said, "The links are over a foot in length, and in weight from 30 to 35 pounds each— they are supposed to be diminished about one- third in weight and size by corrosion."

Most of those links have disappeared, but two of them—perhaps those made from the iron smelted at the Ancram ironworks—are reportedly in the collection of the New-York Historical Society in New York City.

Another link, perhaps from Ancram, too, was recovered off Anthony's Nose in 1861. It is on display under glass in the historical museum on the grounds of Washington's Headquarters in Newburgh.

Many links of the West Point chain have been recovered, but they have no connection with the Ancram ironworks except that they are similar in size and manufacture. A large number are displayed at Trophy Point on the grounds of the United States Military Academy at West Point and at other places.

For more details on the chains, their construction and operation, I suggest an impressive book, *Chaining the Hudson: The Fight for the River in the American Revolution,* by Lincoln Diamant, published by Lyle Stuart in 1989.

What Kind of Products Came Out of the Ancram Ironworks?

In the period from 1749 to 1775 (before the American Revolution)—carriage wheels, stoves, grates, firebacks, mill iron, bolts, share molds, wagon tires, pots, and kettles. In addition, customers for bar iron were able to get square bars, narrow plates, broad flats (used for axe heads), and thin flats.

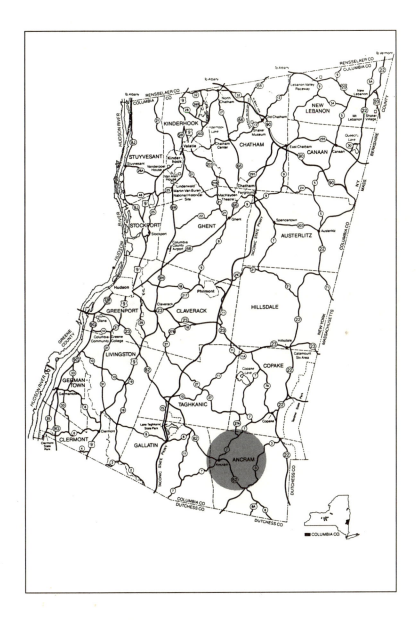

1. Map of Columbia County, showing Ancram at bottom right.
Courtesy of Columbia County Planning Board.

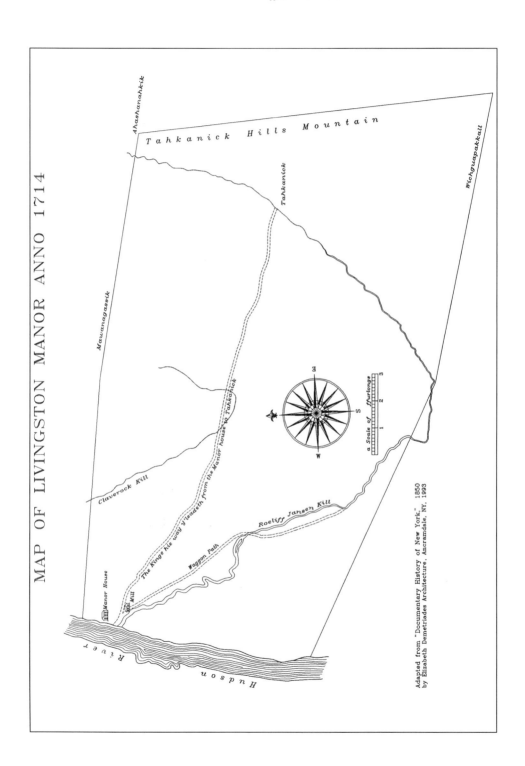

MAP OF LIVINGSTON MANOR ANNO 1714

Adapted from "Documentary History of New York," 1850
by Elizabeth Demetriades Architecture, Ancramdale, NY, 1993

2. This Map of the Livingston Manor made in 1714 is adapted from the "Documentary History of New York," volume III, 1850, where it was printed with the following caption:

At the request of ROBERT LIVINGSTON ESQ. of ye County of Albanie, Lord of the Manor of Livingston, I have measured and laid out for him, said Manor lying and being situate on the East side of Hudson's River on both sides of Roeleff Johnson's Kill in the County of Albany and Dutchess County. Beginning on the East side of Hudson's River Southward from Vastrix Island at a place where a certain run of water waterth out into Hudson's River called in ye Indian tongue Wachankassik, from thence running East by South, three degrees forty five minutes, Southerly nine miles and a half to a certain place called in the Indian tongue Mawanagassik where Indians have laid several heaps of stones together by an ancient custom amongst them, then East by South seven degrees forty five minutes, Southerly nine miles and a half and thirty rod, to a heap of stones laid together on a certain hill called by the Indians Ahashanahkik, by the north end of Taghkanick hills or mountains; then South two degrees West along said hills thirteen miles and a quarter to a place called Wichguapakkall, then East two degrees fifty minutes Northerly and one hundred and fifty-six rod to a run of water on the east end of a certain flat or piece of land called in ye Indian tongue Sakahka, south by east eight dewgrees thirty minutes, Easterly one hundred and forty rod, to five Linds or Lime trees marked with St. Andrews Cross, standing together where two runs of water meet together on ye south side of said flat; then West Southwest six degrees thirty minutes Southerly one mile and a half and twelve rod, to a rock or great stone on ye South corner of another Flat or piece of land called by the Indians Acawaisik, then West Northwest thirteen miles and three quarters of a mile to ye Southermost bought or bounds of Roeleff Johnson's Kill, then Northwest eleven degrees Northerly by eleven miles and three quarters to a dry gully at Hudson's River called in ye Indian tongue Sackahampa opposite to ye Sawyer's creek, and from there up Hudson's river, including all ye turnings and windings therefor to ye first station. The whole being bounded on the South by ye land of Col. Peter Schuyler and ye land of Lieut. Col. Augustin Graham & Companie; to ye North and East by the land of Capt. Hendrick van Rensselaer and ye Patentes of Westenhook, to the West by Hudson's River, containing in all one hundred and sixty thousand two hundred and forty acres.

Performed this 20th day of October 1714.

John Beatty, Dep. Surv'r

3. Links of the Revolutionary War great chain across the Hudson River, similar to those forged at Ancram, on display at Trophy Point, West Point. *Courtesy of Public Affairs Office, United States Military Academy, West Point, N.Y.*

4. The falls of the Roeliff Jansen Kill at Ancram. *Photograph by Brian Yorck.*

5. Erroneous state historical marker, putting origin of mill five years later than it actually was. *Photograph by Brian Yorck.*

6. Philip Livingston, second Lord of Livingston Manor, builder of the Ancram iron mill. *Courtesy of New York State, Office of Parks, Recreation and Historic Preservation, Clermont State Historic Site.*

7. Robert Livingston, third Lord of Livingston Manor, operator of the Ancram iron mill. *Courtesy of New York State, Office of Parks, Recreation and Historic Preservation, Clermont State Historic Site.*

8. Earliest known photograph of the Ancram paper mill. *Superior Facts* magazine.

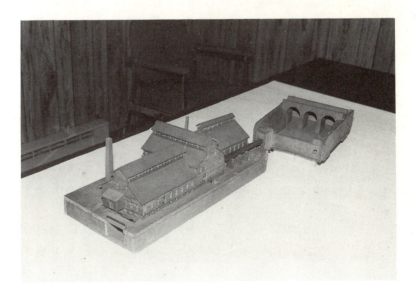

9. Model of paper mill, carved by Henry M. Miller in 1896. *Photograph by Brian Yorck.*

10. Mill workers around 1917-1918. Front row (from left to right): Theodore Blass, Homer Ham, Paul Woodward, Jake Tanner, Florence Tanner Dwy, Suzie Brigg, Carrie Traver Kilmer, Orliea Garrison, Ella Hinsdale. Second row (at extreme right): Harry Blass, Will Neeling, Tom Kennedy, Will Bathrick, Grant Briggs Sr., Dick Scott, Charles McDonald. Third row: Louis White, Lester Carl, Dode McArthur, Walt Hill, Lee Boice, Leroy Blass, Frank Hinsdale, Steve Nagy?, Charles Boice, Sid Killmer. Fourth row: Fred Tompkins, Ward Blass, Earl Wood, Charles Parsons, John Cherrie?, Dewitt Traver. *Collection of Ethel Miller.*

11. Mill workers. Front row: Unknown, Walt Hill, William Bathrick, Unknown, Richard Scutt, Leroy Blass, ? Hinsdale, Charles Boice. Back Row: Unknown, Theodore Blass, Charles Parsons, Harry Blass, Unknown, Unknown, Fred Tompkins, Unknown, Lee Boice. *Courtesy of Kimberly-Clark Corporation.*

12. Four of the early rag-pickers in the mill: Left to right, Orliea Garrison, Florence Tanner Dwy, Ella Hinsdale, Carrie Traver Kilmer. *Courtesy of Kimberly-Clark Corporation.*

13. The Ancram Paper Company Bridge is a three-span stone arch bridge, reportedly built in 1850, according to New York State Department of Transportation records. It is the oldest known bridge in the county. Like the nearby paper mill, the bridge is constructed of Dolostone, a sedimentary rock similar to limestone, but with the addition of magnesium. Dolostone is not found in the vicinity of the mill; a band of it extends for some distance along the Harlem Railroad, and the rock is also found in Pine Plains, from which one variety, the Pine Plains formation, takes its name.

This section of Route 82 is part of the original route of the Ancram Turnpike Company, a company chartered in 1804 by the state legislature to link Salisbury, Connecticut with the Hudson River. President of the Company was Henry Livingston (1753-1823) who had inherited Great Lot 3 of the Manor, then including the village of Ancram and much of the turnpike's proposed route from Ancram west.

It seems most likely that the bridge was built at the time of the construction of the paper mill in 1854. The mill required substantial loads of stone probably delivered from quarries on the east side of Ancram or Pine Plains. It would have been a natural task to rebuild the bridge over the Roeliff Jansen at that time.

3

The Paper Mill: One

By Peter H. Stott

One of the oldest and most significant industrial sites in Columbia County is the original site of the Livingston Iron Furnace at Ancram on the Roeliff Jansen Kill. The furnace, erected in 1742-43, the first in the province of New York, was in use until 1845. In addition to being an important source of cast and wrought iron for the province and the state, it was also an important local employer. Today, however, the most visible aspect of the site is the paper mill constructed in 1854 and subsequently rebuilt.

The Ancram Paper Mill was for many years the largest of the Columbia County paper mills. Like most of them, its usual product in the latter half of the nineteenth century was straw paper, a coarse wrapping paper produced by numerous upstate New York mills from rye straw, a grain which the county excelled in producing. (In 1875, the county produced 17 percent of all the rye grown in the state.)

But the Ancram Paper Mill was not built as a straw mill. Rather, it was the work of two Berkshire County paper manufacturers who planned a large-scale paper mill to produce newsprint from cloth rags. In the 1850s, Berkshire County, Massachusetts, was one of the leading paper manufacturing areas in the nation. Elizur Smith (1812-1889) and George Platner (d. 1855) were already partners in several Berkshire mills. Smith already owned

six paper mills in Lee when in 1853 he and Platner organized the Ancram Paper Company and acquired the old
Livingston iron furnace property.

The mill was built in a cruciform plan, with a main
building 54 by 90 feet in plan, flanked by two wings. The
north wing, nearest the dam, was 57 by 76 feet and housed
the bleaching room. The south wing, 60 by 95 feet, housed
the machine room. The walls were constructed of blue-
stone, a blue-gray dolostone, also used in the nearby stone
bridge. The roof slopes were laid in slate. An 1895 model
survives and shows the original form of this structure.
George W. Linn (1804-1885), a prominent western
Massachusetts mechanic, is credited with supervising the
mill's construction, remaining as superintendent of the mill
until returning to Lee. At Ancram, Elizur Smith is credited
with making the first local trial of ground-wood pulp on a
commercial scale. The experiment was not a success, however, and the bankruptcy of the firm after the financial
panic hit the country in 1857 forced Smith to abandon the
process.

In 1860, the mill was purchased by the parents of
George H. Peaslee and his cousin Samuel Carpenter.
Peaslee (c.1830-c.1912) was the eldest son of the pioneer
Malden Bridge paper manufacturer, Horace W. Peaslee
(1807-1885). Carpenter's father was Horace Peaslee's partner in Valatie, Jeremiah Carpenter. The elder Peaslee was
the owner of several paper-making patents, including that
for the Peaslee straw washer and system for cooking straw.
George had learned the paper-making trade in his father's
mill and soon after the purchase of the Ancram mill, converted the mill to the manufacture of straw wrapping.

The firm was enormously successful in the early
1860s, and in 1867 Peaslee and Carpenter expanded the
mill extensively. To undertake the expansion, the firm was
mortgaged heavily, Horace Peaslee assuming most of the
debt. After the younger Carpenter's death in 1868, the

mills continued to run, but evidently relied on extensive support from the senior Peaslee.

The Peaslee mill is the best example of what was once a major industry for the county. In 1865, the county boasted twenty-four paper mills, a number substantially greater than in any other county in the state. Total capital invested, value of mill property, and number of men employed also substantially exceeded comparable figures for other New York counties.

In 1878, *Lockwood's Directory of the Paper Trade* reported that the Ancram Paper Mill, then one of 27 paper mills in the county, produced 25 tons of straw wrapping paper each week and employed two cylinder paper machines: one with a 72-inch roll and another machine with a 68-inch cylinder; 44 men were employed at the time of the decennial census two years later when it was noted that three water turbines provided 130 horsepower.

After Horace Peaslee's death in 1885, the mill failed, and in 1889 it was sold to settle his estate. The buyer was a wealthy New Yorker, Sigmund D. Rosenbaum. Under Rosenbaum, the mill gave up the straw wrapping paper business, concentrating on light-weight manila papers. The mill was leased to several different parties until 1905, when with several associates, Rosenbaum incorporated the Ancram Paper Mills.

Insurance company plans of the building indicated that the oldest portions of the present structure were rebuilt in 1908, presumably after a fire, although a search of several local papers has not yet revealed such an event. It is clear from an examination of the structure itself, however, that much of the original stone structure survives, visible on the interior and in portions of the exterior's river facade. Significantly, the basement of the structure appears to date almost entirely to the 1854 period of construction, including an early wood-floor "drainer." It is also quite possible that a detailed study of the basement would indicate that portions of the stonework date from the eighteenth-century Livingston iron furnace, incorporated into the paper mill during construction.

The mill changed hands again in 1921 with its purchase by the Standard Products Corporation. For a number of years, carbon and light-weight tissue papers were its products. The mill's equipment was rebuilt, and in 1927 the mill was entirely electrified. A major addition to the mill was made during World War II when Building No. 4, which enclosed the south and southwest sides of the original building, was erected. However, a prolonged two-year strike beginning in 1949 was only ended by the company's sale of the mill in 1951.

The mill was purchased at bankruptcy auction by Peter J. Schweitzer, Inc. in 1955 and used initially for reconstituted tobacco products. The mill became part of the Kimberly-Clark Corporation in 1957 through its acquisition of the Schweitzer company. Much of the older machinery was removed, including line-shafting, the last turbine, and two rotary digesters. One of the two paper machines was rebuilt and started up in 1967 to produce electrical papers. A wastewater treatment plant was constructed on the opposite side of the river in 1970. The same year, and again in 1972 and 1981, the company added warehousing space to the north and south ends of the mill.

Today the company operates two paper machines. One operates nearly full-time producing porous plugwrap, while the second machine operates part-time producing reconstituted wrappers and binders for cigars. Portions of the latter machine, built by Rice, Barton & Fales, date to 1872. The company employs, on the average, approximately 100 persons, and is the largest single employer in this section of the county.

Prepared for *A Guide to the Industrial Archeology of Columbia County,* a forthcoming publication of the Columbia County Historical Society.

4

The Paper Mill: Two

From *Superior Facts* Magazine, 1932

Columbia County's first paper mill was built in 1801 by Pitkin and Edmonds at Stuyvesant Falls, in which writing paper was made by hand. George Chittenden, a practical paper maker from Hudson, N. Y., had charge of the construction and operation of this mill. In 1801 Mr. Chittenden secured another power site which was called Chittenden Falls, now Rossmans, where he built the second mill in the county. He devised most of the mill's machinery and made high-grade, loft-dried writing and bank note paper.

In later years Columbia County produced straw-paper almost exclusively. Although much straw was raised locally, the mills of Columbia County depended largely on neighboring counties for raw material. Large quantities were drawn by team from west of Schenectady. The *Paper Trade Journal*, January 1, 1875, said:

> *"An article in the Commercial Bulletin of New York says that the straw grown in the Mohawk Valley is of superior quality to all others for paper making. It is stiffer, brighter and cleaner and is used largely by paper mills of Columbia County."*

Columbia County strawboard, wrapping, and especially cigarette paper, became noted for quality. Consequently this county, as reported in *Lockwood's Directory* of 1875, had 29 paper mills. [Editor's note: the 1878 directory listed 27 mills.]   With the passing of straw-paper most of these mills have gone out of existence, the 1931 Directory of Lockwood showing only four mills.

THE ANCRAM MILL

This mill is one of the few remaining paper manu-factories in Columbia County. It is situated on what was originally known as the Roeliff Jansen Kill, now commonly called Ancram Creek. In colonial days this site was occu-pied by furnaces and forges, and it is said that they fur-nished their quota of cannon balls for the Continental Army during the War of the Revolution. In fact, excavations for modern improvements have revealed evidence of their pro-duction.

We reproduce the story of the old iron works, as published by Everts and Ensign in their history of Columbia County 1878:

ANCRAM IRON WORKS

"The town of Ancram first derived prominence and notoriety from the iron works erected by [Philip Livingston, son] of the first lord of the manor at Ancram Village, in 1748. [Editor's note: The correct date is 1743.] This was the first, and for many years the only iron works in the colony. The furnace stood on the site of the present paper mill, at the south end of the bleaching room. The top-house was on the north side. There were four forges built at different times—one stood near the furnace, one stood nearly opposite on the east side of the kill, one stood near the dam on the west side, and the other was about eighty rods down the stream on the west bank. The one near the dam was carried away by a freshet in the spring of 1839. The others were torn down, with the exception of the lower one which was afterwards converted into a dwelling.

"The ore used was formerly brought from Salisbury, Conn., in carts, but about 1830-35 they began to get ore from the Copake mine. The ore was first made into pig-iron in the furnaces, and then refined in the forges and made into bars and rod-iron of all kinds. The manufactures of this furnace won a wide reputation for their excellence.

"When running full force the works furnished employment for from sixty to one hundred men, as colliers, teamsters, founders, blacksmiths, etc.

"The iron works remained in the possession of the Livingston family until 1845, when it was sold under fore-closure of mortgage to Peter R. Rossman and Joseph D. Monell. In 1847 Rossman sold out to Monell who held it until 1853, when he sold it to George W. Platner."

ANCRAM'S FIRST PAPER MILL

George W. Platner was, in company with Elizur Smith, operating the Lee, Mass. mills under the firm name of Platner and Smith, and George Linn was superintendent of their Huddle mill (now a part of the Smith Paper Company's Eagle mill). These three gentlemen, together with Stephen H. Platner, a brother of George W., organized the Ancram Paper Company which took over the property, and in 1833 rebuilt the old iron works into a paper mill, making newsprint from rags. Mr. Smith soon withdrew from the organization. Mr. Linn, who was superintendent and who supervised the equipment of the mill, then operated the mill with the Platners under the firm name of Platner and Linn, but he too, in a few months, sold out his interests and returned to Lee.

Mr. George Platner died in 1855 and Stephen Platner, with a partner, Peter C. Conkling, organized as Platner and Conkling and operated the mill for about three years. They became financially embarrassed and in 1860 the mill was sold by foreclosure sale to George H. Peaslee and his cousin, Samuel W. Carpenter, and the plant was then operated under the firm name of Peaslee and Carpenter. Extensive improvements were made in the mill buildings and equipment, and the product was changed to straw wrapping. We reprint the following interesting description of the rebuilt mill and equipment, as published by Everts and Ensign in 1878:

PEASLEE'S PAPER MILL

"This mill was built gradually. The different buildings were erected from time to time during the four years following the sale. In 1864 they rebuilt the dam into a very durable structure. The present proprietor, George H. Peaslee, succeeded Peaslee and Carpenter in 1868, and continues the business. This mill is the largest in Columbia County. The main building, which is fifty-four by ninety feet and two stories high, extends east and west and is flanked by two wings one and a half stories high, the southern wing being the machine-room, sixty by ninety-five feet, and the northern wing, the bleach-room, fifty-seven by seventy-six feet. The buildings are of heavy cut stone and covered with slate roofs. They cost about $50,000.

"The machines (one seventy-two inch, and one sixty-eight inch cylinder) are set upon iron beams supported by iron columns, and produce an aggregate of from twenty to twenty-five tons of wrapping paper each week. The materials used are about thirty tons of straw, five or six tons of lime, and twenty tons of coal each week, and employment is afforded for forty-five or fifty hands. The water is carried from the dam in a trunk three hundred feet long, and furnishes power to run three turbine wheels, one of seventy-five horse-power and two of twenty horse-power each. The fall in the stream is thirty feet at this point. In the bleach-room are eight boiling tubs, or vats, each having a capacity of four tons of straw, and the straw, after bleaching and washing, is ground to pulp in six engines, the roll-bars of which are thirty-six inches in length. The total cost of the buildings and machinery was about $100,000. The real estate connected with the mill consists of about fifty acres, exclusive of the dam and water privilege, and Mr. Peaslee owns about a dozen dwelling houses, occupied mostly by his employees."

This business was evidently financed by Horace W. Peaslee of Malden Bridge, father of George H., and no doubt the large amount of money spent in rebuilding the mill so burdened them with overhead that they could not operate at a profit, and in 1868 Horace H. Peaslee took over the mill. Mr. Carpenter left the organization, but George H. Peaslee continued as manager for a short time after his father's death, when the company went into bankruptcy. *The Paper Trade Journal* of March 14, 1885, published the following:

> *George H. Peaslee, straw-wrapping manufactur-*
> *er, Ancram, N. Y. has assigned to Jacob H.*
> *Duntz, of Gallatinville. The assignment provides*
> *for the payment of two notes of $2,500 each,*
> *held by the Stissing National Bank and indorsed*
> *by Jacob H. Duntz; a promissory note for*
> *$1,000, made to the order of Horace W. Peaslee*
> *and held by the National Bank of Kinderhook;*
> *three bonds and mortgages, amounting to*
> *$10,000, held by the executors of the estate of*
> *the late Horace W. Peaslee, the assignor's fa-*
> *ther. It is said that Mr. Peaslee owes consider-*
> *able in the vicinity of the mill for straw, and the*
> *impression in the trade is that creditors not pre-*
> *ferred will not realize much, if anything.*

These difficulties, however, were settled and John N. Peaslee, a younger brother of George H., managed the business for the estate. An item in the *Paper World* of February, 1886, announced—"J. N. Peaslee now runs the Ancram mill as well as the one at Malden Bridge."

After about a year the Ancram mill was closed. In order to settle the estate the mill was sold September 20, 1889, to Sigmund D. Rosenbaum, a wealthy New Yorker, and it was operated by his son-in-law, S. J. Rose.

An advertisement offering the property for sale appeared in the *Paper Trade Journal* of August 7, 1886, which gives a good description of the property at that time, as follows:

> *PAPER MILL PROPERTY FOR SALE—The Ancram Paper Mill, situated on the Roeliff Jansen Kill at Ancram, Columbia County, N. Y., is offered for sale to close the estate of Horace W. Peaslee, deceased. The depot grounds of the Hartford and Connecticut Railroad Company are located very near, and formerly belonged to this property. The mill has been run on straw wrapping paper, and the well-known brands of George H. Peaslee, 'Export' and 'Regular,' have been manufactured here for twenty-five years. The mill and dam are built of stone; ample water privilege; fall of thirty feet; eight tenement houses; one large and three small barns; about fifty acres of good land; surrounding country is a fine, fertile farming section; large quantities of rye straw easily procurable in the vicinity. Mill contains 8 bleach tubs, 5 iron curb pulp-beating engines, one 'Peaslee straw washer,' three turbine water-wheels, one steam boiler, one lathe with shafting, pulleys, presses, belting, steam and water pipes, etc; two paper machines built by Smith, Winchester and Company (one 68 and*

*the other 72-inch). The property is in fair
running order. Its present capacity is about
forty tons per week. The entire property is
offered for sale at a moderate price. Buyers
are invited to examine this desirable property.
Correspondence solicited. Mr. Hudson, residing
near by, will show the property. For further information and as to price, terms, etc., apply to
Charles M. Hall, 229 Broadway, New York;
George H. Peaslee, Copake Iron Works,
Columbia County, N. Y., or to the undersigned.*
Elizabeth A. Hall,
Administratrix of H. W. Peaslee, deceased,
156 West 53rd St., New York.
(Elizabeth A. Hall was a daughter of Horace W. Peaslee.)

Later Mr. Rosenbaum leased the mill to John
Hoffman, who manufactured manila tissue for about a year.
His son, William, had charge of the business when an explosion of several dryers, caused by the use of high pressure steam, wrecked one of the machines and badly
damaged the building. Isaac Hoffman, who made straw
wrapping in the "Old Stone Mill," formerly operated by D.
P. Ketcham, at Stanfordville, Dutchess County, N. Y., was a
brother of John Hoffman. After the explosion the mill was
leased and operated as the Ancram Paper Mills, with Ross
White as proprietor from 1896 to 1901, and after that by S.
J. Rose and A. F. Frank, who added to the mill's equipment
a Jordan engine and one 1,000-pound heater, and started the
manufacture of anti-tarnish colored tissues and light-weight
specialties. They had offices at 201 Wooster Street, New
York City.

In 1899 Sigmund D. Rosenbaum deeded the property to his wife, Sittah R. Rosenbaum, who in turn deeded it
to the Ancram Paper Mills, incorporated January 10, 1905,
the incorporators being Samuel J. Rose, Alfred Frank,
Jerome W. Frank, Sigmund Rosenbaum and David E.

Openheimer. The mill was improved at this time, and many new lines, including a brand grass bleached tissue and F. O. C. brand anti-tarnish, were featured. In 1908 the mill was rebuilt and the 72-inch Fourdrinier was widened to 90 inches.

In 1921 the business was taken over by the present organization. The mill and equipment were rebuilt and today it is one of the most efficient plants making light-weight paper in this or any other country. Completing the improvements in 1927 the mill was entirely electrified, all the improvements having been made without shutting down or loss of production, surely a record and a tribute to the ability of those in charge.

The present organization operating the Ancram Paper Mills consists of Charles Campbell, president; J. A. L. Miller, vice-president; C. Matthews, secretary. The mill is equipped with one 72-inch Fourdrinier, with Edwards attachment, manufacturing 5,000 pounds of technical tissues and specialties. Their New York office and sales rooms are at 152 West 22nd Street.

ANCRAM MILL WOOD MODEL
The photograph of the model of the Ancram mill was secured from Harry M. Miller, of Ancram, N. Y., who carved the model by hand in 1896. Mr. Miller operates a hardware store in Ancram and in making the model of the Ancram mill he could stand on the porch of his store and get an excellent and clear view of the mill. The model is considered an excellent reproduction of the mill in every exterior detail.

GEORGE W. LINN
The first superintendent of Ancram mills was George W. Linn. He was born in 1804 and when a young man started work for William Clark and Company in

Northampton, Mass., making fine papers, and the first paper for United States postage stamps. In 1840 he went with Platner and Smith in their Turkey mill at Tyringham, Mass. He was later superintendent of their "Huddle mill" and went with them to equip and start the Ancram mill. When he left Ancram he returned to Lee and in 1856 organized, with Benjamin Dean, the firm of Linn and Dean, making hand-made bank note. Mr. Dean retiring, Elizur Smith purchased his interest and the mill continued under the name of George W. Linn and Company. Mr. Linn was later associated with P. C. Bayard. The mill was later sold to the Bairds and afterwards became the property of the American Writing Paper Company.

Mr. Linn retired from business September, 1869, and went to live with his daughter in Germantown, Pa., where he died April 6, 1885.

The next superintendent of the Ancram mill was Peter Conklin, who was in company with Stephen Platner.

It is most probable that George Peaslee superintended the mill during the time it operated under his name.

William Hoffman was superintendent during the time his father, John Hoffman, had the mill leased.

After Hoffman, Henry McArthur, who learned the business at the Ancram mill, was the next superintendent, and remained until 1905. He died in 1908. His son, Henry McArthur, is now millwright.

William Pusey went to work in the Ancram mill, superintending the rebuilding of the mill in 1905-1906, but left before it was again making paper.

E. J. McHUGH

The next superintendent was E. J. (Edward) McHugh, who was born in 1866, and got his first paper-making experience at New Hope, Pa., in the Union Paper Mill Manufacturing Company's mill, originally operated by

Welch and Miller. He afterward worked for the Diamond Mills Paper Company at Bloomfield and Millburn, N. J., and then at the Passaic Mill, Franklin, N. J., which was operated by Joseph and Richard Kingsland, inventors of the Kingsland refining engine. From there he went to the National Fibre Board Company at North Leominster, Mass., where he superintended the installation of a Fourdrinier machine and started it up making tissue papers.

Mr. McHugh next went to the Eagle Mill of the Smith Paper Company at Lee, Mass., leaving there in April 1907, to become superintendent of the Ancram Mill which he changed over from toilet and wrapping tissues to the manufacture of carbon and other high grade lightweight papers. He operated this mill successfully until his death in 1922.

John McHugh, born August 11, 1893, and son of Edward McHugh, took his father's place and now acts as general superintendent, with Frank Hinsdale as foreman. [Editor's note: in 1932.]

JOHN A. DECKER

One of the noted paper makers of the past generation, John Ambrose Decker, was born June 24, 1837, at Ancram, N. Y., the son of William H. and Gertrude Spencer Decker. He was educated in the common schools at Ancram and obtained his early paper making experience under George W. Linn. Going to Lee, Mass., Mr. Decker became superintendent of the Smith Paper Company's Valley Mill. After the East Lee flood of 1880, Mr. Decker purchased the ruins of the old Washington Mill and rebuilt it of brick. Thomas Sabin became associated with him and the firm of Decker and Sabin was formed. The mill was operated for two years, after which Mr. Decker became superintendent of the Springdale Paper Company at Westfield, Mass.

From there he moved to Berlin, N. H., as superintendent of the Glenn Manufacturing Company, which was later acquired by the International Paper Company. He was also superintendent of the Ivanhoe Paper Company at Paterson, N. J., the Ontario Paper Company at Brownsville, N. Y., and the Rumford Falls Paper Company's mill. When the Great Northern Paper Company built their mill at East Millinocket, he took charge and operated it for three years, after which he retired, making his home in Dixfield, Maine, until shortly before his death in January 1912, at Pittsfield, Mass.

WILLIAM H. DECKER

William H. Decker, a son of John A. Decker, was born in Lee, Mass., May 22, 1886. He learned the business under the instruction of his father, and later became the first superintendent of the St. Regis Paper Company. He was later a paper expert in the employ of the Solvay Process Company at Syracuse, N. Y.

Reprinted from *Superior Facts* magazine, a publication of the Paper Makers Chemical Corporation, February, 1932.

Women Employees

An experiment in using women workers in the mill began sometime in the 1890s, but there is very little information available on why it started, how it worked, and why it ended. The only clue is a short report in the Ancram notes of the *Pine Plains Register* of June 3, 1893, which read:

> *"After being closed for a week to make needed repairs, the paper mill started up again on Tuesday. The experiment of employing female help in the finishing room has been tried for a short time but for some reason failed to reach the desired result as nearly all the employees have sought other employment."*

The mill has no records today indicating what happened.

5

The Mill Today

By Jeffrey Holmes

Financial problems of the Thin Paper Company closed the Ancram Mill in 1953. It had been shut down suddenly when the Central Hudson Power Company cut off power. This left all its tanks, pipe lines, and paper systems full of wood pulp, and it was reported that paper was still festooned on the paper machine drying cans. It must have been a sad day as the workers left a cold, dark, and silent mill.

As with any community that loses its major employer, the closing of the mill affected many families. Out of this concern, Hoysradt (Mike) Porter, Ancram's postmaster and general store proprietor, formed a Citizens' Committee in order to try to find a new owner and operator. Other members of this committee were Vernon Dwy, Ed Parsons and John Steihle.

The mill property ownership had reverted back to the Standard Products Corporation of New York City, which had run the mill since 1908. James G. Buckman, Standard Products' vice president, worked with and encouraged Mike Porter's group in its search for a new owner. During this time, Ed Parsons and John Steihle "carried the clock" as watchmen for the mill's insurance carrier.

The Citizens' Committee became very active in early 1955 with Mr. Porter writing to every possible paper company trying to find someone interested in opening the mill. The amount owed in back property taxes was about $13,000, which was in addition to the mortgage debt of

$65,999.86. A sheriff's mortgage auction was set for June 7, 1955, at 2 p.m. at the Columbia County Courthouse in Hudson, New York.

With the coming of the auction Mike Porter continued soliciting companies that might be interested. Of special note are letters received from Braunstein Papers and Ecusta Paper Company, both competitors of the current owners, which indicated no interest in the property. In fact, Fred O. Fleming of Braunstein recommended turning the mill into a commercial laundry. One of Mike Porter's letters did hit home, though. It was to the Peter J. Schweitzer Paper Company of Elizabeth, New Jersey.

Peter J. Schweitzer, a Russian, had moved to New York City from France and in 1908 established a firm which imported cigarette paper. The Schweitzer family owned cigarette papermaking facilities in Southern France. During World War I, the shipment of cigarette paper supplies from France to the United States was interrupted. This led Peter J. Schweitzer to conclude that the United States should have its own source of cigarette paper. In 1920 he bought a two-paper-machine paper mill in Jersey City, New Jersey and started his own U. S. operation.

Peter J. Schweitzer had five children—Louis, Sarah, William, Elizabeth and M. Peter. He sent his two oldest sons, Louis and William, to the University of Grenoble in France and to the University of Maine and Columbia, respectively, and then, to learn the business, they interned at the family's paper mill in Malaucene, France. Thus, when Peter J. Schweitzer died in 1922 at the age of 47, his two sons, Louis, then 23, and William, then 21, were able to assume responsibility for the business. Peter J. Schweitzer was incorporated in 1923.

Louis and William were good businessmen and continued their expansion in the tobacco industry throughout this century. At first it was difficult for U.S. tobacco companies to accept the new American cigarette paper as they were used to the French material. In order to bridge this gap, the Schweitzers used their thin papermaking abilities to research and produce an ultra-thin, non-conductive paper to be used in the condenser/capacitor industry.

From the mid-1920s up until the mid-1980s, when capacitor paper was replaced by plastic films, the Schweitzers were the world's foremost producers of this paper (some of which was produced in Ancram). In order to meet demand for both cigarette and condenser papers, as well as carbon and business forms paper, the Schweitzers acquired mills in Elizabeth, New Jersey (1929), Spotswood, New Jersey (1940), Mount Holly Springs, Pennsylvania (1941), Lee, Massachusetts (1950), and Ancram (1955). In the early 1940s the remaining Schweitzer brother, M. Peter, joined the family-owned business after having practiced law in New York City. Thus, Peter J.'s three sons had taken what their father had started and developed it into a premier specialty papers business for cigarette, condenser and business papers.

Part of this success was based on the innovations that Louis and William introduced. Flax as a raw material for cigarette paper and a process for the reconstitution of tobacco leaf wastes were significant advances. The conversion of scrap tobacco into a sheet of paper was William's main interest in the early 1950s. He had learned that some of the cigarette companies were adding to the virgin tobacco blend a sheet cast from the by-products of tobacco-leaf processing called homogenized tobacco. About one-third of a tobacco leaf grown for the manufacture of cigarettes resulted in unusable by-products, including stems, dust and flakes. These by-products, which were 100 percent tobacco, could be formed together in a sheet, using a casting process called homogenization, by the addition of various binding agents.

Since the Schweitzers were already major suppliers to the cigarette industry and had become proficient paper-makers, William Schweitzer wondered if a tobacco sheet could be made on a paper machine from the tobacco by-products. Paper was made from fibers, and experiments showed that there was sufficient fiber in the tobacco-leaf waste materials. Further, a homogenized sheet without non-tobacco agents would be preferred by the cigarette companies. The Schweitzers needed another location to develop this new idea and found what they sought in Ancram. On June 7, 1955 they bought the two-machine Standard Products Corporation mill at a sheriff's sale for $53,000. It was the last mill purchased by the Schweitzers.

The participants in the auction were M. Peter Schweitzer and Roy Plaut, Sr., the family and business attorney. Plaut's son, Roy, Jr. was working for the Schweitzer paper mills at the time. In fact, Roy, Jr. continued to work in the Schweitzer mills and became president in 1982. Judging from the price, there was not much interest in the mill at the auction.

On the drive back home to New York City along the Taconic Parkway, Roy Plaut, Sr. asked Mr. Schweitzer what he would use as a name for the business when he drew up the legal documents. M. Peter Schweitzer thought for a moment and said that the name of the road they were traveling would be appropriate and thus the Ancram paper mill became the Taconic Paper Company.

The mill had been purchased to provide a place where William could develop the reconstituted tobacco paper process. The condition of the mill was a papermaker's nightmare. The mill had gone down cold in 1953 and it took six to seven months just to clean up the chests, lines, and tanks that had been left full of wood pulp stock. During this time, Vernon "Ditty" Dwy and Charlie Tanner acted as watchmen. Workers were hired, equipment cleaned up, and new equipment installed in preparation for the tobacco paper trials.

Some of the local Ancram papermakers rehired were John Steihle, who had been a mill manager during Standard Products operating regime, Roy Boice, Bill McCue, Talcott Benton and Cliff Boyles. In addition, tradesmen and papermakers were brought in from the Lee and Spotswood mills. Leroy Palmer, an electrician, Norman Buck, a carpenter, Ken "Shep" Shepardson, a machinist, and Matt Mountain came from Lee, Massachusetts. Veteran papermakers Clayton Travor and Ray and Ralph Young came up from the Spotswood, New Jersey mill. This crew came under the direction of an experienced papermaker, Nathan Flaxman, who was brought in from the Elizabeth, New Jersey mill. He worked for the next three years in Ancram developing the tobacco reconstitution process.

Experiments to produce a tobacco sheet had been started in Elizabeth on its No. 4 paper machine. Burley tobacco stalks had been successfully used to produce a paper sheet that could be used in the cigar industry to hold the smoking tobacco column as a binder and/or as an overwrap of the cigar, called a wrapper. Attempts to make a cigarette filler tobacco at Elizabeth were unsuccessful. Thus the decision was made to start fresh at the Ancram Mill site.

To make a sheet of paper out of 100 percent tobacco fibers was quite a challenge. For one thing, tobacco scraps have very little strength in their fibers and do not lend themselves to a continuous papermaking process. Also, tobacco has 40 percent soluble materials which must be captured in order to give the paper sheet tobacco character.

The solution the Schweitzers eventually found was first to extract the soluble portions from the raw material, separating them from the fibers. While the fibers went in one direction, first to be refined and then made into a sheet of paper, the extracted solubles (extractables) went another way to be concentrated. Then, as the sheet left the paper machine for final drying, the concentrated extractables were re-introduced into the sheet in a specially designed size press.

The sheet at this point was heavy, weak, wet and tacky. The solution to drying this sheet, the problem first tackled at Elizabeth, was found in a so-called "tunnel" dryer. The dryer, wide enough to accommodate the full sheet and heated by hot air, worked by carrying the sheet on a series of slats or tubes. Thus supported, the sheet could shrink without tearing as it was being dried. At the end of the process, the sheet was cut into pieces approximately the size of a human hand, packaged, and returned to the cigarette manufacturers in the same wooden barrels ("hogsheads") in which the raw material was received.

The total process was known as the two-step paper-making process, and eventually was called the Schweitzer process. Also, because of the differences between this process and the other cast, or slurry, process, the finished product was termed "reconstituted" tobacco as opposed to "homogenized" tobacco.

It had taken three years to develop the process at Ancram, but the 100 percent tobacco, non-additive product was very successful. The machine on which the tobacco was produced eventually became labelled as Number 20, but it soon became apparent that the output of this pilot operation was insufficient to supply the demand for reconstituted tobacco leaf (RTL). A decision was made to build a new, large machine at the Spotswood, New Jersey mill. Known as Number 16 machine, it was installed in 1958 and has been producing RTL for the U. S. cigarette industry ever since.

In addition to the U. S. operations, the Schweitzers built an RTL factory in France in 1963 (LTR Industries) to supply European cigarette manufacturers.

Just two years after the formation of the Taconic

Paper Company, which was part of Peter J. Schweitzer, Inc., the Kimberly-Clark Corporation acquired the company. At that time the Schweitzer family became large Kimberly-Clark stockholders, with William Schweitzer and M. Peter Schweitzer serving on the Board of Directors. The direction for the Schweitzer Mills remained under the people who were in place and up until the mid-1980s the French and U. S. tobacco-associated mills were still known as the Schweitzer Division.

The colorful Schweitzer history was made possible through the efforts of three resourceful brothers: Louis, William and M. Peter. Known equally well as businessmen and philanthropists, each had taken the responsibility for major stepping stones in their company. Louis was perhaps best remembered for his innovation in making cigarette paper from American grown flax. William's most memorable achievement was developing reconstituted tobacco for the cigarette and cigar industries. And the purchase of the Lee, Massachusetts mills and phenomenal expansion into the capacitor tissue and film markets came from M. Peter's impetus. Louis and William died within six months of each other in 1971. M. Peter currently resides in California.

It is people who make successes happen and Mike Porter's Citizens' Committee proved that a few local people could make a difference. They had found a new owner for the Ancram Mill. The day after the sale Mr. Porter wrote the Standard Products Corporation with a list of Ancram area workers requesting employment. In James G. Buckman's response letter, he thanked Mr. Porter:

June 10, 1955
You have been very thoughtful and of benefit to your community for the letter you have sent out to prospective buyers. We are enclosing herewith, our check in the amount of $50 as a tribute to you for the performances you have engaged in.

Mike Porter turned down Standard Products' offer to recommend him for employment, saying his position of postmaster and proprietor of a small general merchandise store was enough.

As noted, William Schweitzer started his tobacco development work with a mix of local people, experienced tradesmen from Lee, Massachusetts, and papermakers from Spotswood, New Jersey. He turned to his right-hand man in paper development, Nat Flaxman, who, along with a scientist named William Selke, developed the Schweitzer reconstituted tobacco papermaking process. Mr. Flaxman was a tireless, dedicated employee who would often sleep in a "broke" (wastepaper) pile waiting for the next step in a machine trial or paper grade development.

Shortly after starting the development work, a resident mill manager named Irving Earle was hired. He had worked for Canadian Glassine and was a Syracuse Pulp and Paper School graduate. Mr. Earle was almost a one-man show, running the mill from one end to the other 24 hours a day. He had early help from Ed Happ, a maintenance foreman, Ed "Mutt" Parsons, who was the mill's purchasing agent and shipper, and Henry Albright, who handled personnel. Mr. Earle took Nat Flaxman's developments and turned them into commercial products and was totally responsible for the manufacturing process.

In 1958 Kimberly-Clark took the reconstituted tobacco filler (chopped tobacco for cigarettes) business to New Jersey, building a new machine at the Spotswood Mill. This left reconstituted tobacco cigar wrappers and binders for the Ancram Mill. This paper, which was wound into narrow rolls or bobbins, was sold to the cigar industry. Little cigars like "Between the Acts" and "Winchester" were quite popular and the business successful. In fact, prior to the Cuban embargo, tobaccos from Cuba were processed through the mill. At times armed agents from the

Bureau of Alcohol, Tobacco and Firearms would stay at the mill to ensure these tobaccos were processed into paper.

Another product, "headtape," was developed. This material was a wet-strength, tobacco-like sheet which was used as a mouthpiece inside a cigar and allowed U. S. cigar smokers to "chew" on them.

The cigar industry was really not large enough to support the Ancram Mill so by the mid-1960s Kimberly-Clark looked to convert the remaining idle paper machine (Number 21) to an electrolytic capacitor paper machine. Demand was high for this grade, which could not be met by the Lee, Massachusetts and Mount Holly Springs, Pennsylvania mills. Electrolytic paper required very clean water and was very thin.

Victor Blache from Lee assisted in the start up (1967) and running of this paper. He sent to Lee for steel calendering to use at Ancram for slitting the paper into small bobbins. Some of these papers were as thin as five ten-thousandths of an inch for ten stacked sheets. This non-conductive sheet was used to separate two electrodes, usually aluminum foil, in a capacitor, a device used to store an electrical charge. The Schweitzer paper mill group was the world's foremost producer of this paper until the late 1970s and early 1980s, when technology passed the paper condenser by.

Irving Earle had seen the Ancram Mill through to the point of full operation. During his time as mill manager, he used slow times to help the community. Mill workers were instrumental in constructing the town's park swimming pool and lighted baseball diamond. They also were no strangers to the volunteer fire department and helped to construct its headquarters.

The mill ran quite well into the late 1960s until a day called "Black Friday," when a corporate officer named Charlie Petzold carried out a management reduction program. Mike Gallenberger was named the new manager for the Ancram Mill; Irving Earle stayed on for a few more years as production supervisor before retiring. Gallenberger instituted many of the modern papermaking practices and policies used by Kimberly-Clark. These included a new wastewater treatment plant that ensured good stewardship of the 700,000 gallons per day of water used and returned to the Roeliff Jansen Kill.

The capacitor paper business was softening and it was decided in 1973 to upgrade the Number 21 paper machine to manufacture the Winchester wrapper little-cigar sheet. This product, sold to R. J. Reynolds Tobacco Company, was very popular at that time. Don Stanton from Lee followed Irving Earle as mill superintendent with Dick Hansen as maintenance supervisor. Ken Hamm, Jim Wellington, Bill Mellan, Ron Van Tassel and Dave Parsons have all served as shift supervisors since 1973.

It was in 1973, when Mike Gallenberger and Don Stanton moved on to the Spotswood, New Jersey mill that a young engineer from Spotswood came to Ancram as mill manager. His name was Edward Ochtman and he was to manage the mill for sixteen years before retiring in early 1991.

During this time, the mill continued to move into the modern era. As capacitor paper continued to decline a new product was developed for the Number 21 paper machine called "porous plugwrap," later trademarked POROWRAP™. Cigar wrappers and binders continued to be manufactured on the Number 20 machine. In 1977 the Number 21 was again rebuilt to manufacture porous plugwrap. This marked the end of the production of electrolytic papers at the Ancram Mill.

The full-time production of porous plugwrap again fully geared the Ancram mill production to the tobacco industry. This new product was a special filter paper that was used to wrap the cellulosic fiber that makes up a cigarette filter. What made Kimberly-Clark's filter paper unique was the fine control of paper porosity, the amount of air that passes through a defined area of paper. By controlling this air flow, the cigarette companies realized they could also control the tar and nicotine levels smokers received through a cigarette.

The method used was to put or punch (using lasers) tiny holes in the paper that attaches the filter (wrapped in plugwrap) to the cigarette paper tube which holds the tobacco. The holes allowed air to pass into the filter (the amount of which is controlled by the porosity or air flow through the plugwrap), thus diluting the smoke. This development has led to the creation of low-tar and nicotine cigarettes manufactured throughout the world.

For a brief period between 1977 and 1979 Ed Ochtman went to the Lee Mills, and Frederick C. Hartwell came from Lee as mill manager. Ed returned in 1979 and through the 1980s and early 1990s brought the mill into the computer age.

The Ancram Mill had developed as its specialty the making of specialty paper. The mill had earned the reputation of being able to make any unique type of paper used in a smoking article. Being the only mill in the world making cigar wrapper and binders using the papermaking process still did not take up all the machine time available on Number 20 machine. So this available time was used for product development. Some unique paper sheets made out of natural and man-made fibers for both the tobacco and specialty paper businesses were developed and commercialized.

POROWRAP™ plugwrap papers continued as productive and profitable products for the mill with a new raw materials warehouse added to the south end of the mill in 1972 and a new finished goods warehouse added to the north end in 1981. New converting equipment was installed in 1982 which allowed a full-width 88-inch wide roll to be slit into individual one-inch wide bobbins all at the same time.

Ed Ochtman completed his tenure by seeing machines installed with computerized process controllers—the tobacco machine in 1989 and the porous plugwrap machine in 1991. The computers, with sensor and controllers, measure the physical properties of the paper and then analyze and control various manufacturing systems that control the quality and uniformity of the paper products. Upon the retirement of Edward Ochtman at the beginning of 1991, Jeffrey E. Holmes was transferred in as the fifth mill manager of the modern era. He had been Number 18 machine superintendent at the Greylock Mill in Kimberly-Clark's Lee Mills group.

During the last 37 years there has been good leadership, but it has been the local men and women of Columbia and Berkshire counties who have contributed their physical and mental energies to produce superior quality products. Their attention, dedication, and work ethic has won hard-fought success for the Ancram Mill. Among them were:

Purchasing — Bernie Parsons, Larry Heath
Personnel — Kathleen Walsh, LaVonne Brown
Finance — Tom Gagne, Rich Greene, Dorothea Hotaling
Maintenance — Ray Hotaling
Engineering — Ron Loring, Roger Wilson
Quality — Colin Walker, Randy Atkins
Manufacturing — Gerry Simons, Dave Parsons,
        Shelt Waldorf, Charlie Williamson, John Cahalen,
        Leon Serra, Tom Hotaling, Ron Hansen
Clerical — JoAnn Elliott, Paula Hansen, Jane Holdridge,
        Joan Wishon, JoAnn Smith, Caroline Garbarini,
        Marge Boothby

Today the mill enjoys the success of the investment by a supportive corporation, a partnering union, a flexible workforce, and good, old-fashioned pride.

In 1992 the Ancram Mill produced a total of over 10 million pounds of product.

In 1875 *Lockwood's Directory of the Paper Trade* listed 29 paper mills in Columbia County. Today there are only two. Today it takes a specialty paper mill participating in a special niche market to continue to survive in a small town in the unfriendly-to-industry Northeast.

Back in 1853 Elizur Smith and George W. Platner, who owned and operated a large group of mills in Lee, Massachusetts, saw papermaking potential in an old iron foundry and forge in Ancram. They built a paper mill there and that alliance and partnership continues today under the Kimberly-Clark Corporation. A paper mill for 140 years and a mill site for 250 years is a proud manufacturing tradition that continues in the mill on the Roeliff Jansen Kill.

ANCRAM MILL MANAGERS (1956 - 1993)

Irving V. Earle (1956 - 1969)
Michael J. Gallenberger (1969 - 1973)
Edward Ochtman (1973 - 1977)
Frederick Hartwell (1977 - 1979)
Edward Ochtman (1979 - 1991)
Jeffrey E. Holmes (1991 - Present)

ANCRAM MILL UNION PRESIDENTS
(1956 - 1993)

(United Paperworkers International Union AFL-CIO Local No. 1479)

Clifford Boyles (1956 -1958)
Byron Scism (1958 - 1961)
Jacob S. Miller (1961 - 1964)
Edward Benton (1964 - 1966)
Daniel R. Thomas (1966 - Present)

The Mill Staff (1993)

Paul Albers	Thomas Gansowski	Barbara Morrison
Tammi Albers	Caroline Garbarini	David Muniz
Arnold Albright	James Garbarini	David Parsons
Leonard Albright	Richard Goodacre	William Parsons
Randy Atkins	Yvonne Graves	Jack Proper
Gaetano Balestra	Paula Hansen	Randy Proper
Michael Barton	Ronald Hansen	Thomas Riell
Patrick Boice	Larry Heath	Larry Rockefeller
Marjorie Boothby	Nickie Heath	Carol Sass
LaVonne Brown	Jane Holdridge	James Schuster
Scott Bruno	Jeffrey Holmes	Leon Serra
Richard Brusie	Dorothea Hotaling	David Silvernail
Gary Bryant	Franklin Hotaling	Kevin Silvernail
John Cahalen	Howard Hotaling	John Skelley
Charles Clough	Raymond Hotaling	Jo Ann Smith
James Clough	Thomas Hotaling	Stephen Spear
Martin Clough	Alton Hoysradt	Richard Stang
Arthur Coleman	Daniel Hoysradt	James Stickle
Christopher Collins	Michael Kachuba	Robert Streeter
Charles Conto	Ralph Kilmer, Jr.	Wayne Swart
James Coons	Roger Kilmer	Stanford Taft
Patrick Corbett	Manfred Klee	Daniel Thomas
Aaron Damon	Charles Lewis	Ronald Van Tassel
Fred Damon	Frederick Link	Killian Waldorf
James Decker	Ronald Loring	Sheldon Waldorf
William Dickinson	Careen Martin	Colin Walker
Andrew R. Dietter	Kathy McBroom	Douglas Weaver
Douglas Dietter	John McCarthy	Donald Wheeler
James Dumas	Earl Mellan	Robert Williams
Ronald Dwy	Howard Miller	Charles Williamson
Jo Ann Elliott	William Miller	Roger Wilson
Cody Elmendorf	Keith Morey	Joan Wishon
Donald Funk	Willard Morey	James Wolcott

14. Aerial photograph of mill, 1973. *Collection of Margaret Porter.*

15. Aerial view of the mill, 1988. *Courtesy of Kimberly-Clark Corporation.*

16. Hoysradt (Mike) Porter, chairman of the Citizens Committee that saved the mill in 1954-55. *Collection of Margaret Porter.*

17. The mill today. *Photograph by Brian Yorck.*

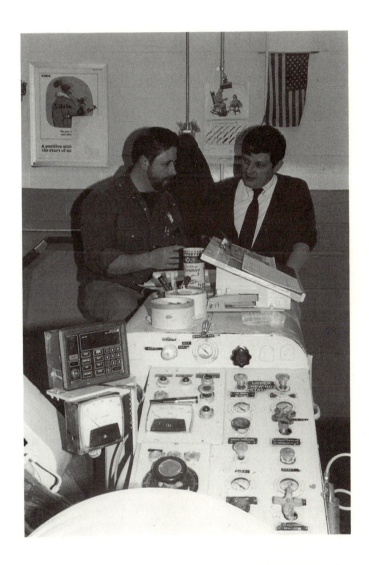

18. The mill manager, Jeffrey E. Holmes (right) confers with one of his supervisors, Sheldon Waldorf. *Photograph by Brian Yorck.*

19. Preparing the mixture for cigar wrapping. Pat Corbett
loading tobacco stems. *Photograph by Brian Yorck*.

20. Preparing the mixture for binder paper. James Stickle loading chalk filler. *Photograph by Brian Yorck*

21. Christopher Collins checking tobacco stems before the paper-making process. *Photograph by Brian Yorck.*

22. David Parsons inspecting the tobacco paper as it comes off paper-making machine. *Photograph by Brian Yorck.*

23. Alton Hoysradt and Katy Ann McBroom preparing the tobacco paper for slitting. *Photograph by Brian Yorck.*

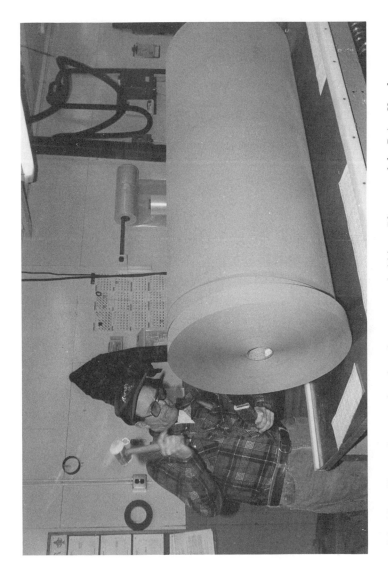

24. Alton Hoysradt separating the tobacco paper bobbins. *Photograph by Brian Yorck.*

25. Arnold Albright supervising removal of cigarette filter
paper from paper-making machine.
Photograph by Brian Yorck.

26. Danny Hoysradt (right) and Scott Bruno and Keith Morey (left) removing finished bobbins after slitting cigarette filter paper. *Photograph by Brian Yorck.*

27. Tom Gansowski at computer control of the paper-making machine. *Photograph by Brian Yorck.*

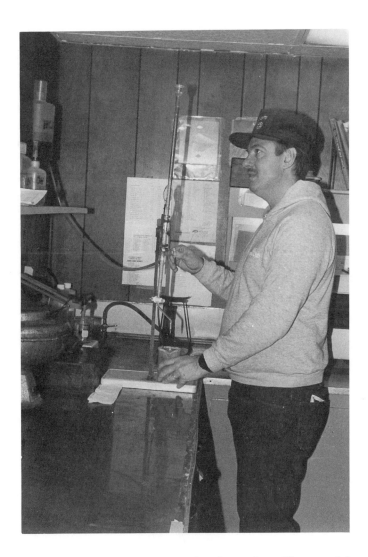

28. Paul Albers in the laboratory, testing the product. *Photograph by Brian Yorck*.

29. Marge Boothby in the laboratory, testing the product.
Photograph by Brian Yorck.

30. Jeffrey E. Holmes inspecting the product before it leaves the mill. *Photograph by Brian Yorck.*

31. Mill scene, Bill Morey. *Photograph by Brian Yorck.*

32. Mill scene, William Dickinson. *Photograph by Brian Yorck.*

33. Mill scene, Jim Wolcott. *Photograph by Brian Yorck.*

34. Mill scene, Roger Kilmer. *Photograph by Brian Yorck.*

35. left: Mill scene,
Daniel Thomas.
*Photograph by
Brian Yorck.*

36. right: Mill scene,
Dorothea Hotaling.
*Photograph by
Brian Yorck.*

37. left: Mill scene, Bob Streeter. *Photograph by Brian Yorck.*

38. right: Mill scene, Joan Wishon. *Photograph by Brian Yorck.*

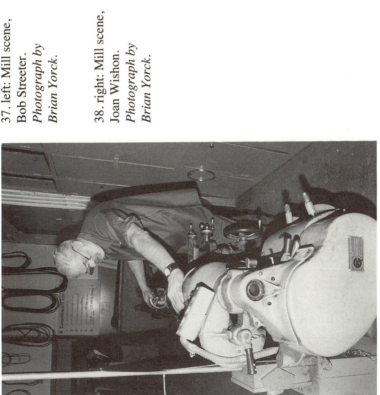

6

A History of Ancram

By Hilary Masters

All records indicate that the town of Ancram came into official existence on March 25, 1814 after having been formed originally by the Livingston family as Gallatin about a dozen years earlier. The name was derived from the Livingston homestead in Scotland, Anchoram,* and the new town in the southeastern corner of Columbia County comprised some 27,000 of the total 160,000 acres the Livingston family had held in what later was Columbia County since the initial grant by the English Crown in 1686.

This semi-feudal manorial system under which it held title to the land was not disturbed by Britain when it ruled the colonies nor was it changed, in the case of the Livingstons, the Van Rensselaers and the Schuylers, by the convention in Philadelphia in 1776, but continued until 1852 as an unhappy remnant of the new Republic's past history and similar to another unsavory tradition the Founding Fathers did not resolve: the issue of slavery. The leasehold system had great importance to Ancram's development and character.

Briefly, the manor system was used by the Dutch government or its agents as an economical and quick means of colonizing their part of the New World. Wealthy men (Kiliaen Van Rensselaer, the progenitor, was a diamond

---

*There are various spellings of Anchoram, such as: Anchram, Ancrum, Ancram. For the sake of convenience the spelling Ancram will be used throughout this book.—ed.

merchant) were granted huge tracts of land along both sides of the Hudson River which they would manage for a profit to the Dutch West India Company. This transfer of land often came as news to the resident Indians. Immigrants, in return for their passage to the New World, would agree to work the land and settle the territory but the length of their tenancy was more than they thought it would be. As tenants on the manors, they paid "rent" to the manor lords in cords of cut wood, bushels of grain and corn, sheep, labor on the master's immediate grounds and acreage and, even down to the 1840s, the old medieval annual fee of "four fat fowles" which prompted historian Samuel Eliot Morison to wonder what, in those days before freezers, the Livingstons did with all those chickens. It was not uncommon for the tenant farmer's rent payment to leave his own table bare and his family begging from others.

On his side of the bargain, the lord of the manor would build roads and mills, adjudicate disputes, garrison a militia for protection against the wilderness dangers and generally keep a patronizing eye and arm around the tenant's welfare and destiny. In actuality, the system perpetuated an archaic relationship that was only slightly removed from outright slavery. The holding and development of large tracts of land were basic to both, and in only rare instances did a manor lord ever sell any of his land to a tenant, even if the latter could put together enough capital for the purchase. Moreover, the tenants could sell their "leases" to another tenant but in all cases the manor lord even got a portion of the sales price, sometimes as much as a third of it. Nor did the wild, unknown nature of that early wilderness encourage many to go elsewhere and after a while, the very human sense of "home," no matter how grim, probably held them too; especially if ancestors who had worked the same land were buried out by the corn patch. So the tenants were forever tenants, generations of tenants, and in fact, some agreements assured the manor lord the land would be worked by "three lives" of one family.

The Livingstons received their grant not from the Dutch West India Company but from James II of England in 1689 after the English took over the New York Colony from the Dutch. A report in 1702 to the English trade commissioners gave the Columbia County lord bad marks for the condition of his farms and their poor income, and it was thought a fresh supply of workers would improve the level of husbandry. Protestant Queen Anne of England was looking for a refuge for a number of German Palatines, her former mercenaries, who now sought refuge from the vengeance of the Roman Catholic French. A large number were shipped over as new leaseholders for Livingston Manor.

Mostly they settled on the west bank of the river, but the town of Germantown in Columbia County indicates some started farming there. It is uncertain how many were sent into the Ancram area. In any event, the Germans were troublesome from the beginning and almost immediately took issue with their relationship with Livingston manor. Some were unhappy that they were given only free beer and bread in return for which they were supposed to make tar and other naval stores for Her Majesty's Navy, and when the land they thought they had been promised turned out to be let out only under the most usurious terms, it took a detachment of the Governor's militia to cow them. But the grumbling persisted down the decades.

There is some suggestion that the Dutch put down a small settlement earlier in Ancram on the banks of the Roeliff Jansen Kill, named from an early Dutch official, but it was small and temporary. The first important settlement took place just north of the village of Ancramdale, around the sharp cap of Croven Hill, and this area was originally called Scotchtown for many years, in tribute to the origin of its settlers, and later Ancram Centre.

It was in Ancram Centre that Robert Livingston, Jr. fulfilled one of his rights and obligations by building a grain mill on the Punch Brook in 1775. The Punch Brook flows in a northerly direction, eventually joining with the Roeliff Jansen, and on this stream in the village of Ancram the Livingstons had already built an iron forge in 1743. The installations on these two streams, together with the development of ore and lead mines later suggest that the most productive application of the old feudal manor system in Ancram was the development of the town's natural resources rather than agriculture.

The iron forge in Ancram was the only one of its kind in the New York Colony and later became important to the new nation as an early "defense plant" for it was in the Ancram forge that cannon balls for the Continental artillery were made as well as links for the great chain that was stretched across the Hudson to keep the British fleet from West Point. Iron ore for the forge was first hauled from Salisbury, Connecticut, by oxcart over the Taconic Mountain Range but later large deposits were discovered at the Weed Orebed near the Copake line and another discovery, the Morgan Mine two miles east of Ancramdale, was opened by the Livingstons in 1776. An old superstition claimed mineral deposits underground generated heat so the discovery of iron ore in this one area gave the name of Hot Ground to the village now called Ancramdale. Punch Brook received its name about the same time due to a farmer, so goes the legend, returning from the stores with a keg of whiskey in his wagon. Going over the rocks of the stream's ford, the wagon rocked, the tailgate gave way, and the barrel of liquor tumbled out to smash on the rocks; *ergo* Punch Brook.

The hostility of tenant for landlord never abated, and it was particularly bitter against the Livingstons, who had the reputation of being "hard masters." In 1811, the tenants of Columbia County even petitioned the Legislature to review the legitimacy of the Livingston claim, but the family's political influence was still strong and there was no review, no change. In Ancram in

1755 an event took place that suggested all was not happy on the old leasehold. A group of Massachusetts militiamen "invaded" Ancram and seized several residents as captives who apparently put up little resistance and may have even encouraged their "capture."

There had been disputes between the two colonies of New York and Massachusetts over the border between them. New York claimed the Connecticut River as its eastern border and Massachusetts looked to the Hudson River as its western line. This would have wiped out the Livingston claim in what is now Columbia County (Massachusetts had no leasehold system nor would it recognize one) and, incidentally, free the land to the tenant farmers *in situ*. So during that raid by the sheriff's posse, perhaps some of the residents of Ancram may have thought they were being liberated rather than made captive.

About ten years later, in 1766, a similar engagement was fought over the iron forge, but the common cause of the Revolution put an end to such disputes and smothered much of the hostility, though Morison says that many of the tenants in the Hudson Valley sided with the Tory cause as their masters, the Livingstons, Schuylers and Van Rensselaers, supported the Revolution. On the other hand, the Ancram Free Ground, the small cemetery a couple of miles south of the village of Ancram, contains the remains of 16 men of the community who served with the American Continentals and with the cannon balls and other armaments manufactured in the Ancram forge it might be said the Revolutionary spirit was not in short supply. The names on the graves at the Free Ground and Vedder Cemetery are some that are very familiar today, such as Ham, Miller, Lasher, Snyder and Coons, among others.

It is safe to assume the tenants on the old manor estates felt that the successful cause of the Revolution would effect some change in their standing with the hereditary lords of the manors. But such was not to be the case in

Ancram or further north since these ruling families, as mentioned before, had had the foresight to back the winning side. Moreover, every time an official document was drawn up in those days, some Livingston was putting his signature to it, from the original Stamp Act Congress down to the Declaration of Independence and the Constitution, so they were in a good position to thwart any motion to change their domains. In other words, the Revolution stopped here.

The town of Ancram was fairly prosperous. The iron forge employed as many as a hundred men sometimes, and there were associated industries set up around it on the banks of the Roeliff Jansen: blacksmiths, saddle and harness makers, shoe cobblers. The grain mill in Ancram Centre also continued to grind corn and flour and there were little businesses being established. Stores began to appear, a grist mill and a saw mill were built in Ancram on the east bank of the Kill by a man named Coons. So perhaps there was too much to do during this period for the antagonism caused by the old rent-laws to come to the surface.

It was also a time for building. Churches were established throughout the area in this first half of the nineteenth century. Ancram Centre built the first one, the Methodist Episcopal in 1847. Two years later, St. John's Lutheran in Ancram and the Presbyterian Church in Ancramdale (Ancram Lead Mines) were built. Simultaneously with the founding of the churches was the establishment of several hotels in the area, suggesting that needs other than the spiritual were being looked after. Two hotels were built in Ancram in 1845. The Ancram Hotel was erected on the site where Peppe's Restaurant now stands; the original structure burned in 1929. Down the road to the east, the Sunnyside Hotel was built in the same year and remained in the same place until fire took it in

1971, when it was called the Ancram Hotel. Ancramdale, or Hot Ground as it was known then, had a hotel as early as 1836 that was called the Phoenix Mines House. It later was bought and run by the Pulver family, being then called Pulver's Hotel. The structure still stands in the hamlet. Post offices were also established during this period: Ancram in 1826, Boston Corners (then still part of Massachusetts) opened its post office in 1828 and we might assume that Ancram Centre's office opened about the same time. In the village called Hot Ground, not only did the residents get a post office in 1838, but the village also got a new name.

Around 1808, according to the *History of Columbia County*, a tenant farmer named Frances Keefer invited some of his neighbors to a "stone bee." Keefer's farm lay near the Punch Brook within the village known as Hot Ground. The "stone bee" was the communal means early farmers used to clear their fields of stones before cultivation. As the story goes, Keefer and his neighbors were walking his field picking up rocks and stones, prying others from the earth with the help of oxen, when the farmer noticed one of these unearthed rocks had a peculiar color. It turned out to be lead and the lord of Livingston Manor exercised his feudal right over minerals and water and leased the mining privileges from the farmer. The mine was opened and Livingston worked it for about ten years, letting it go idle until 1836 when it was sold and reworked, and in 1838, with the opening of the new post office, the name was officially changed to Ancram Lead Mines. In March of 1930 it was changed once more to Ancramdale.

Schools were among the first considerations of the inhabitants after the Revolution. A year after Ancram-Gallatin was created by John Livingston, he leased out a small parcel of land for the establishment of a school. This was in 1804 and the school building still stands in Smoky Hollow; it is now a private home.

Ebenezer Kingman and Allen Sheldon were listed as the trustees of the new school system in Ancram, for which they paid the lord of the manor a dollar per year for the land and one of those chickens the Livingstons seemed fond of collecting. The state law of 1812 established the free school system and the town of Ancram was divided up into districts each with its little one-roomer, many of which still stand but deep in the gloom of brush and wild growth. In the village of Ancram one of them has been renovated and has become the official town hall.

A carriage works was built in Ancram and stores in Ancram and Ancramdale began to show such names as Porter, Niver, Hoysradt and Tremain on their inventory lists. There was also a store in Ancram Centre and one of its keepers at this point of history, also the postmaster of Ancram, gave part of his name to a slang term, still used by some residents in referring to the area, which returns this review to the subject of the leasehold system and its history in Ancram.

As the protests against the rent paid out to the lords of the manor became more violent in the 1840s, a John A. Rockefeller of Ancram Centre became known as one of the champions of the anti-rent cause. Since he was not only a storekeeper and postmaster, but also now owned the grain mill built on the Punch Brook in 1775, it might be assumed that he was not a tenant farmer but a freeholder, of which there were many in the area. It is recorded that several meetings of the anti-rent faction were held at his house and Mr. Rockefeller was one of the first men in the area to switch his allegiance from the Democratic Party to the newly formed Republican Party, a symbolic shift made by a great number of the peasantry mainly because it was felt that the Democrats in the State Legislature and the Governor, Silas Wright, had not supported the anti-rent cause sufficiently. The term "black-republican" is still used in certain areas to describe a citizen's degree of partisanship, and in the mid-nineteenth century half of the term was applied to Mr. Rockefeller, the other half of the epithet formed from his name: Black Rock. Ancram Centre, where this mill owner and friend of the anti-renters as well as early Republican party members lived was called *Black Rock*, and is still called that by older residents of the community.

There were men like John A. Rockefeller arising throughout the area and the days of the freehold system were growing shorter in the 1840s. Two natural catastrophes overtook the Livingston estate in Ancram; in 1839 a flood on the Kill swept the iron forge away and in 1843 fire destroyed the handsome mansion they had built across from the forge. The house was rebuilt by Livingston heirs a few years later and still stands, having recently undergone extensive renovation.

But in 1839, a greater catastrophe befell the Livingstons than the loss of their manor. This was the death of Stephen Van Rensselaer, who left some $400,000 in back rents to be collected from his tenants. Van Rensselaer apparently had not collected from his tenants because of idleness rather than from benevolence, for he left strict instructions in his will for the arreared rents to be collected and it was the attempt by his heirs to make these collections, backed by sheriff's posses and even the state government still influenced by the lords of the manor, that brought the whole system down. The details of this final climax of what was known as the "Anti-Rent War" is better covered elsewhere (*Tinhorns and Calico* by Henry Christman is recommended). It was a reformation, finally by violence, of the old system that probably should have been changed at the beginning of the new Republic. It provoked curious alliances and even stranger opinions. For example, as might be expected, James Fenimore Cooper and Washington Irving might side with the manor families in the confrontation since these two writers served and were served by the establishment of their day; but Walt Whitman, America's great poet and paradigm of libertarian philosophy, drafted harsh editorials against the "rabble" anti-renters in his post at the *Brooklyn Daily Eagle*.

Aside from John "Black Rock" Rockefeller, there are few individuals from Ancram specifically named in the history of the struggle nor were there any significant encounters here as there were in neighboring Taghkanic, Hillsdale or Copake. However, given its history and other incidents, it's reasonable to assume that the cause of the anti-renters was generally supported in Ancram. The final blow was struck against the manor families by the State Court of Appeals in 1852, which held that the Van Rensselaers could not collect their rents and, to their credit, the Livingstons seemed to have accepted the verdict of the court and history and retired to their galleries and verandas to muse on the haze on the Hudson and the sun setting behind the Catskills.

By 1845 they had lost the Ancram forge by a mortgage foreclosure, and it was converted and re-built as a paper mill in 1854, which it has remained to the present, the current process manufacturing cigar wrappers and other tobacco products. The grain mill in Ancram Centre had been sold, the lead mines had closed down; so the Livingston family in 1852 had more or less passed out of Ancram's history as an effective force. Almost simultaneously, something new and rather startling took its place. This new force had the power to change population centers, reform the use of the land and open up the world to the people of Ancram. Indeed, when it came into Ancram, it shook the land as if those old stories about Hot Ground were true, as if the heat generated below the ground surface were about to geyser. And, in fact, fire and steam did accompany this new historical force, for it was in 1852 that the railroad first rolled into Boston Corners.

The building of the railroad into that northeastern village of Ancram also brings the story of Boston Corners into this review, since that triangular, 1,000-acre tract was still a part of the State of Massachusetts until this time. The old survey lines had virtually isolated the community from the rest of Massachusetts because of the high rise of the Taconic Range between them, and this natural wall to the village's east also made it difficult for Commonwealth authorities to travel to Boston Corners. Law and order were not easily maintained and, since New York State officials had no authority there, the community became a sort of no-man's land, open as a refuge for ruffians and other unsavory types. The decent citizenry tried their best, petitioning the State of Massachusetts to cede the area to New York, but what must have spurred their efforts even more was the arrival of the railroad and an event that took place in Boston Corners a year later, in 1853.

Boxing was illegal in those days and the great matches were held in foreign places or even on barges and boats. Since no state authority effectively enforced the law in Boston Corners, it became known as a safe place to stage these contests. With the construction of the Harlem Railroad through Boston Corners from New York City in 1852, the place became a boxing promoter's dream. The fight on the books was the one between "Yankee" Sullivan and John Morrisey. Ten thousand sports fans arrived on the new railroad and practically took over the small village of Boston Corners for two days and a night. According to reports, every chicken, pig and lamb was slaughtered to feed the horde and Boston Corners' one hotel, every barn, front porch and back field bedded them at night. It must have been a frightening experience for the residents of that community. The next day, after the brawl, some of the mob "persuaded" station agent William Van Benschoten to flag down a freight going south for the trip back to New York City. Not because of, but certainly influenced, by the chaos caused by the community's ambiguous status, the State of Massachusetts ceded Boston Corners to New York in May 1853, and it was accepted in July. Congress ratified the transaction in January 1855 and the Town of Ancram formally annexed the community on April 13, 1857.

As for the fight, it apparently was one of those brutal blood baths of the day that went 37 rounds in 55 minutes with John Morrisey the winner over Sullivan, whom he outweighed by 30 pounds. The champion of Boston Corners went on to become a state senator from Saratoga and is also credited with conducting the first meeting of thoroughbreds at the Spa.

In all there were three different railroads built through Ancram, and these lines of steel laid down through the hills and across the stream beds of the community shaped and reshaped the destinies of the town's people as had the Punch Brook and the Roeliff Jansen Kill channeled the early history of Ancram. After the Harlem Railroad built its track through Boston Corners in 1852 (only recently closed down as part of the bankrupt New York Central), it took 20 years for the next roadbed to be laid into the town of Ancram, and parts of this roadbed can still be seen winding through the woods and fields south of the village of Ancramdale. Starting from Pine Plains in 1868, the Poughkeepsie, Hartford and Boston Railroad Company, also known as the Poughkeepsie and Eastern, began extending their line through the then-named village of Ancram Lead Mines and on to Boston Corners to junction there with the Harlem Railroad for north-south service. Perhaps the initial motivation for the railroad's construction was to service the ore mines located in the area, because the new line took over four miles of track already put down to

Boston Corners from an iron ore mine that had been discovered east of the village in 1855. The Reynolds Orebed sometimes mined as much as 10,000 tons of ore per year. The new railroad also built two large trestles to service the flag stops of Halstead and Tanners on the way. The Poughkeepsie and Eastern opened service to Ancram Lead Mines (Ancramdale) in 1872, thereby stimulating a surge of business enterprises in that community, and it is not entirely coincidence perhaps that the community of Ancram Centre closed its post office in 1871.

Three years later, in 1875, the third railroad was built into Ancram and again probably to service the ore deposits in the area. This last company was the Rhinebeck and Connecticut which entered the village of Ancram from the west and followed the Roeliff Jansen Kill in a circuitous route to junction again in Boston Corners, making stops in Ancram and the Weed Orebed along the way. This iron mine, one of the earliest in the town, was a very large operation and was situated in the northern part of town. Some of it lay in Copake, and remained active up until the turn of the century.

All this railroad activity coming into Boston Corners made the village a very important junction center, and timetables of that day indicate a continuous shunting and shuttling of trains around the clock. Station agents were maintained on a 24-hour basis and the clicking of the old telegraph key is still a familiar sound in the memories of residents. The trains generated numerous businesses. The Vosburgh family presided over a hotel and store as well as coal yard and market. A carding machine and cloth dressing plant was established and great stock pens were built near the tracks to keep cattle and sheep prior to their shipment to the slaughterhouses in New York City. Photographs of the rail yard at that time indicate a large and sophisticated complex.

In the village of Ancram the paper mill also expanded and was served by the new railroad service, but the irony of history changed the nature of the raw material that the railroads had sought to freight from something taken from beneath the earth to a product manufactured on the gently rolling meadows of the town's surface. For the Reynolds Iron Mine closed down in 1875, the Morgan Mine a year later (the Ancram Lead Mines had been closed since the end of the Civil War) and the Weed Orebed lasted only a few years more.

It all began in 1872 when Jacob Miller, then the town supervisor, took eleven cans of milk down to the station in Ancramdale and shipped them to Boston Corners and from there to New York City on the Harlem line. Miller had been carrying his milk by wagon to Boston Corners for shipment, but the new railroad was only a mile from his farm on what is now called Crest Lane.

This service also benefitted other farmers, some of whom had not been able to get to Boston Corners with their produce. That first shipment of milk by Supervisor Miller from Ancramdale was the beginning of a relationship between the farmers of Ancram and the railroad that was to last nearly seven decades and which transformed the nature of farming there.

Under the old manor system, agriculture still generally relied on medieval methods. Implements and tools were rather crude and, most important, the attitudes of the tenant farmers toward the productivity of their farms were not encouraged by the onerous rental of the leasehold. Diversified farming was still the usual method after the farmers assumed ownership of the land, and it was not until after the establishment of the convenient rail service from Ancram and Ancramdale that the large dairy herds familiar today became as much a part of Ancram's landscape as are the fertile grasslands they graze.

With more and more farmers taking up the specialization of dairy farming, milk plants were set up in both villages to receive the white "ore" these new walking mines of Ancram were producing. In Ancramdale, the first receiving plant was built in 1896, just across from the railroad station, and both buildings stand today. In Ancram, R. F. Stevens & Company set up a receiving and bottling plant that handled more than 100 cans of milk daily; Willowbrook Dairy took over this facility later. A bottling plant was built in Ancramdale, and both of these facilities employed many men in the township, sometimes with shifts working around the clock.

New businesses were established and clustered around this activity generated by the railroads. Mr. Niver, who already had a store near the Ancram Lead Mines station, decided to build another one a bit away, and did so in 1871 next to the existing Pulver's Hotel, thereby creating the nucleus of the village of Ancramdale as it is seen today. In Ancram, George Woodward and the Bachmans set up as blacksmiths and carriage builders. Peter Miller had a tin shop. The Peaslee Paper Mill developed a process to manufacture paper from straw which gave the local farmers another cash crop. In 1889 the mill changed ownership, and Sigmund D. Rosenbaum began the manufacture of manila tissue; about a half a ton of it turned out daily and was shipped on the Rhinebeck and Connecticut. Henry McArthur was the last local manager. John Porter had built his first store in 1858, and was the postmaster of Ancram as well, thereby initiating a dual service to the community that is part of the Porter family tradition. Strever and Hills also ran a store as did Jay Woodward and William J. Edelman toward the end of the century. This last establishment was built by the Simons family in 1928 and has been recently restored under that name. Down in Ancramdale (Ancram Lead Mines) an apple jack distillery was established and there were other small businesses around the store and hotel. The mill in Ancram Centre, built by the Livingstons and now owned by Eason Card, continued to grind corn and grain for the farmers.

The Civil War had been fought and the names of 114 men from the town of Ancram who had joined the ranks of the Union Army joined the list of those who had fought for the Republic and were buried in the Free Ground. The town gave more of its men to the nation's wars up to and including the conflict in Vietnam, and in May 1961 the Ancram Athletic Field was dedicated to the memory of Sergeant Wallace T. Blass who was killed on the island of Luzon, the Philippines, in World War II.

In 1901 an enterprising young man named George Card, a cousin to the mill owner, started the first telephone system in town, and the central switchboard was located in his parents' home, a house that was made into the Pond Restaurant a few years ago. Electricity took a bit longer, 1924. All of these changes came rather rapidly and were largely due to the appearance, and the prosperity it brought, of the railroad. Moreover, passenger service afforded by the lines connected the residents of Ancram with any part of the state, the country, even the world. Contemporary residents afflicted by the bankruptcy of the rail system and general break-down of mass transportation would be very envious of the timetables and the great choice of travel arrangements available to their grandparents. All points of the compass were accessible from Ancramdale or Ancram. For just one example, passengers could board the 7:20 A. M. in Boston Corners, change to the New York Central in Poughkeepsie and be in New York City at 11:22 A. M. Or if a more gracious mode of travel were desired, at Poughkeepsie transfer could be made to a dayliner, steaming either north or south on the river. Arrival in New York would be at 5:30 P. M. or in Albany at 6:10 P. M. There was also a variety of express services for those in a hurry. The mail came by rail and was efficient and quick.

On June 3, 1910, a slim young man took up a place on the round stone step before Pulver's Hotel in Ancramdale and talked about his hopes of being elected to the New York State Senate. He lost the senate race but he went on to become governor and then president, for his name was Franklin D. Roosevelt. Some older residents of the town claim it was Roosevelt's first public political speech, but whatever the qualification, there's no doubt he did speak here on that date at the invitation and introduction by an old friend, William E. Edelman. Years later, Mr. Edelman received a personal invitation to attend that first inaugural from President-elect Roosevelt.

However, Jacob H. Hoysradt was elected to the state assembly from Ancram in 1893, after having served as supervisor and town clerk for several terms. These were the names of Ancram—Hoysradt, Miller, Edelman, Porter, Smith and Barton—that were building the town and farming its lands, shaping its character to the point it is known today.

In 1938, after almost 70 years of operation, the railroad made its last shipment to Ancramdale, a carload of fuel to the Barton and Hoysradt store. This partnership had taken over the old Niver Store around 1902; the Barton family also bought the Pulver Hotel next door in the 1920s. Both the Poughkeepsie and Eastern and the Rhinebeck and Connecticut stopped their trains through the different parts of Ancram in 1938 and their disappearance once again transformed the community, but not with the same effect as when they had chugged into view in the 1870s. The mill in Ancram, then owned by Standard Products, continued in operation and the village did not suffer as much as did Ancramdale, the difference being made by the new mode of shipping milk.

The milk manufacturers found it more practical to ship the milk by truck rather than rail, so large trucks would

pull up at the receiving and bottling plants in the two villages and transport the local product directly to the market
area. The railroad, no longer having this profitable shipment on its freight schedules, ceased operating and the
tracks were torn up before World War II and, so legend has
it, joined the scrap of New York City's Sixth Avenue ele-
vated line shipped to Japan's war industries. Ed Card,
grandson of Eason, continued to do custom grinding of
grain in the Punch Brook Mill until 1940, and the paper
mill in Ancram, the old forge of 1743, passed under the
management of Peter J. Schweitzer Company, currently the
Kimberly-Clark Corporation. From its first days under the
old manor family up to the present time, the mill-forge has
been and still is the major industry in the community, often
extending benefits to the people of Ancram far beyond the
issuance of a payroll. Many of its managers are remembered fondly for their interest in Ancram and their volunteer service in the town's behalf, and among these, perhaps
the name of Irving Earle might be singled out for special
remembrance.

But in Ancramdale, the picture was much different.
The old hotel had become an apartment; the blacksmith
was gone, as well as the meat markets. The two stores had
been reduced to one; Smith's store had sold out and then
been closed down. Prohibition probably finished off the
apple jack distillery. However, still in operation was the
milk plant, and even though the milk was being picked up
by truck, it was still being handled and bottled in
Ancramdale. The plant in Ancram had closed almost immediately after the R & C Railroad had stopped running;
so, farmers as far away as Taghkanic would bring their
milk to Ancramdale to the factory, some even by horse and
wagon as late as the 1940's. But then the Ancramdale plant
closed down in 1954 because of a new development in the
storage and transportation of raw milk: the bulk tank.

With the installation of one of these new tanks, around 1955, the individual farmer didn't even have to take his output to the local factory for trucking, because a truck would pull right up to his barn and siphon off the milk. So the receiving and bottling plant no longer had a purpose and it closed.

The Barton and Hoysradt General Store held on for a few years more and together with the post office inside it and the Presbyterian Church were the last of the energetic enterprises that had marked the village of Ancramdale. In 1961 the store closed down after an auction of its goods, hardware and supplies that is still talked about by those who attended it. The post office was moved across the street to where one of the old meat markets had been and it seemed as if Ancramdale might join Ancram Centre as a community that existed only in the memories of old-time residents. The small school houses of the Ancram system were closed and the students apportioned between the two centralized school districts of Pine Plains and Roe Jan. New people moved into the area to work and to retire. However, the dairy industry continued to prosper and expand, though the enormous size of today's farm would astound the old tenant farmers of the last century. Their size, complexity and investment of capital is even astounding, in some cases, by today's standards.

About ten years after it went out of business, the Barton and Hoysradt store was bought and reopened as the Ancramdale General Store. Mr. Charles Rudnick, in one swoop of investment and paint brush, transformed the center section of the village of Ancramdale overnight, renovating the old hotel, the store, and several annexes. There is even a genuine carriage works in operation, building or repairing those beautiful vehicles of another year for people who, because of the energy shortage or nostalgia, wish to hitch up a horse instead of turning an ignition key. Similar but more extensive restorations are being made in the village of Ancram by Messrs. John Peter Hayden and Donald Chapin. Simons Store has been restored by them as has the old Livingston manse across from the mill, the old Grange Hall and several other buildings and houses. Where the blacksmith and harness-maker shop once stood is now the Ancram Grog Shop. [Editor's Note: Unfortunately, by 1993, the carriage works in Ancramdale and the Grog Shop in Ancram had ceased operations.]

The land remains as it always lay, and the Punch Brook and Roeliff Jansen still join together to make their way through the shale and gravelly loam of the soil. The mill in Ancram continues to turn and there is a peace out by Halstead, disturbed only by a loon or cry of a fox, that is related to the stillness before the railroad clanked across the trestle. Cattle low in the distance and children laugh and shout as they scramble from yellow buses on the modern hard-surfaced roads. The town is prosperous and peaceful these days, content and at rest, as though it had paused and were waiting for whatever new development of man or history might pass through the village countryside.

* * *

In the 1980s, Ancram was discovered by people with money. Attracted by its rural charm and proximity to metropolitan New York, they began to buy up its dairy farms and divide them, thus accelerating the transformation of Ancram from a major farm community to one of large and sometimes elaborate rural residences.

The Hoysradt farm, a bicentennial farm, went, although Pat and Helen Hoysradt remained in the area. Bob Podris's Crest Lane Farm, sold to a group of English investors, went out of business in the great Federal buyout of 1985. Crawford Bryant, Bill Lutz, Bob Podris, Jr., Lou Fish and Frank LaCasse sold their cows. By 1989, there were only 12 working farms left in Ancram—fewer black and white Holsteins in the fields and barns.

Although some farm operators started to mine gravel from their fields, others diversified in more bucolic ways. On the Millerhurst farm—the oldest farm in Ancram in continuous operation—where Harold Miller and his sons continued to milk cows, Emily Miller started a greenhouse and nursery. Down Wiltsie Bridge Road on the old Thompson-Finch Farm, Marni and Don Maclean started to farm organically, growing apples, strawberries and vegetables. On Snyder Road, Art and Susan Bassin raised a huge horse barn for a major Arabian horse-breeding operation.

In Ancram as elsewhere, environmental concerns mounted in the 1980s. Forced to close its only landfill in 1988, Ancram joined Gallatin in operating a transfer station for garbage. In 1989, faced with convoys of trucks hauling construction refuse and debris into the town, Ancram passed a law banning such dump sites. In a concerted effort to clean up the town early in 1989, 293 abandoned cars were hauled away.

Escalating land prices made home ownership for young people quite difficult. But the influx of well-off newcomers also offered opportunity. David Boice started a home-care and estate maintenance service. Perry Miller's bull-dozing operations boomed. Patrick Hoysradt soon had a dozen more men working for him building new homes.

Regulation of proposed new large-scale development—some with cluster housing—emerged as the major problem for Ancram as it approached the 21st century. How could it maintain its rural charm while permitting landowners to divide more land for sale to more newcomers? Part-time public officials, most of them unpaid, wrestled with the problem constantly. By 1989, in an effort to maintain open space, Ancram began to rewrite its master plan, sub-division regulations and zoning laws to try to control its new growth.

Despite these problems, grass turned green each spring, the Roeliff Jansen Kill rolled merrily on to the Hudson River, alfalfa fields bloomed into lush green, tractors trudged across fields leaving large tan rolls of hay in the summer and fall, deer continued to bound—and Ancram, despite its problems of residential growth, remains, at least for the time being, an oasis of visual beauty and serenity.

Reprinted from *A History of the Roeliff Jansen Area*, a publication of the Roeliff Jansen Historical Society, 1992.

The First Superintendent

The first superintendent of the paper mill in Ancram was George W. Linn, a prominent mechanic from Western Massachusetts, who supervised construction of the mill in 1853-54. He was born in 1804 and died in 1885.

Ancram Town Officials (1993)

Supervisor	Gerald Simons
Town Council	James Bryant, Andrew Dietter, Patrick J. Hoysradt, Robert Podris
Town Clerk	Diane Boice Yorck
Assessors	Clifford Campbell, Jr., chairman; Terry Bryant, Douglas H. Dietter
Assessment Review Board	Baxter Stickles, Jr., chairman; Frank Bitel, Doris Faber, Henry Hoysradt, Rosalie Rothvoss
Tax Collector	Jane N. Holdridge
Town Justices	Eugene Aleinikoff, Brian C. Yorck
Highway Superintendent	John W. Slater
Planning Board	Joan Taylor, chairwoman; Peter Adler, Barry Chase, Donald Maclean, Emily Miller, Kathleen Osofsky, Fred Schneeberger, Dennis Sigler
Zoning Board of Appeals	Harold Faber, chairman; Thomas Diaz, Jordan Katz, Daniel Rothvoss, Sheldon Waldorf
Building Inspectors	James Butrick, Allen Bell, deputy
Youth Commission	Jennifer Boice, chairwoman; Sharon Cleveland, James Cole, Kenneth Frink, Dorothy Lutz, Christopher Lutz, Westley Slater
Fire Commissioners	Ernest Sigler, chairman; John Derrick, Perry Miller, Tom Miller, Paul Waldorf
Fire Company	James Bryant, president; Brian Yorck, vice president; John Derrick, secretary; Fred Schultz, treasurer
Fire Department	David Boice, chief; Dennis Boyles, first assistant chief; Willard Morey, second assistant chief

Slaves at the Mill

Among the workers at the Livingston iron forge at Ancram was at least one black slave. In the early 1750s, there was a blacksmith named Coffio, his wife named Princess, a slave couple named Tom and Mary, and a boy called Jack, son of Mando. The women may have served as domestics at the Livingston house and the men, other than Coffio, were either domestics or laborers. One task of the slaves at Ancram was to deliver articles from the manor store to the storehouse near the furnace and the forge sites.

7

A Biography of Roeliff Jansen

By James Polk

The Goddess of History is a tricky muse. She can hide her course under a canopy of myth, legend, folk tale, and possibly invention, often displaying only the biased account of a single contemporary observer to serve as gospel simply because there is no other record. Or she might offer some such slanted version as source material for whole generations of historians and then, after the volumes of secondary works have piled up, have it totally debunked by some new manuscript discovery from the dismal recesses of a dank and dusty library.

Roeliff Jansen, the man for whom this area of New York State is named, sometime sailor, sometime farmer, sometime government official, is one offspring of this most fickle mistress. By myth, a man whose influence extended through the whole colony of New Netherlands, by legend, a pioneering explorer and by local folklore, the first European resident of this area, Jansen was really none of these things. Instead, he seems a fairly average individual whose life saw successes and failures in about equal measure and whose passage is marked by nothing so much as the plain ordinariness of it all.

Born about the year 1602 on the island of Marstrand off Goteborg, Sweden, his early life remains a thing of mystery to would-be investigators; probably it was spent like most others from the island in the booming coastal

trade among Scandinavian countries in the business of her-
ring fishing for which his homeland was then famous.
Before he was twenty, however, young Jansen found his
birthplace too confining for his dreams and so, again like
many others, emigrated to Amsterdam in search of fame
and fortune. He found neither, although he did manage to
meet and marry the vivacious and much pursued Anneke
Jans, a charming woman rapidly growing into the belle of
the busy port city. Still, material wealth continued to avoid
him, and after barely a decade in Amsterdam, Jansen decided once again to move on.

This time the family (there were also two daughters
and Anneke's mother, Tryn Roeloffs) made a much grander
move: on March 21, 1630 they boarded the workhorse of
the Dutch West India fleet, the *Eendracht*, in the harbor of
Texel and set off for New Netherlands. This new journey,
as befitting Roeliff's greater maturity, was not taken entirely on speculation, for he carried a contract from Kiliaen
Van Rensselaer to farm a plot on the latter's vast but as yet
unpopulated domain near the present city of Albany. As
helpers for this task, also on the *Eendracht*, were Claes
Claeson and Jacob Goyverson, two Norwegian sailors like-
wise in search of fresh beginnings in the New World. The
terms from Van Rensselaer called for a salary equivalent to
$72 per year in exchange for which they were to transform
an untamed wilderness into a profitable farm.

After a lengthy but apparently uneventful passage
the *Eendracht* docked in New Amsterdam on the 24th of
May and the would-be farmers immediately transferred
their belongings to a small "krag" or yacht, the basic unit of
transport on the Hudson, which would carry them upriver
to their new home. On board were many others with the
same destination for this was the first group of settlers dis-
patched by the patroon to his new colony of Fort Orange,
and there was lots to be done. Shelter had to be built from

scratch, for there was none; the land had to be cleared and tilled before it could be planted, for it had never seen a plow; communication downriver with New Amsterdam and with other Dutch colonies in Delaware and New Jersey had to be established, for as yet there was nothing beyond the river itself.

The Jansen farm, called "de Laets burg" took time to get in running order and, not surprisingly, the men and women of the little party spent the first two years of their residence struggling to make a go of their new lives, not making their presence felt in the growing little community but fighting to carve some sort of existence out of nothing. Finally, by June 1632, the land began to surrender its wealth to the persistent farmers. By the end of that month Kiliaen Van Rensselaer, who always managed to keep close watch on his possessions even from his desk in Amsterdam, reported that Jansen had prepared five morgans (about ten acres) for sowing with winter wheat and was readying additional acreage for future planting. As a measure of his confidence in the farmers at de Laets burg, the patroon also sent them some cows and hogs purchased from Gerrit de Reux to add to the four horses and eleven sheep already in their possession so that they might have, as he put it, "a complete farm." The only complaint over the way things were going in the New World to be heard from Holland, in fact, was directed more at the colony itself than at the activities of a single property. The land which Jansen had laboriously cultivated for winter wheat, it seems, could not then be planted for want of seed, a lack placed squarely on the shoulders of the officers of Rensselaerwyck; the patroon fired off an angry letter to his agent in charge lambasting the management of the colony for permitting such a failure. But as for Roeliff Jansen himself, he remained in the lord's good graces and on the first of July, 1632, he was given the oath as "schepens" by Rutger Hendricksz van Soest.

The exact nature of this post is unclear; apparently, the schepens served as some sort of agent between the patroon and his tenants. Although the word has been translated into "magistrate," the oath of office was to the lord (Van Rensselaer) and not to the state, meaning that it was probably more of an enforcing than a judicial nature. Whatever the exact duties, the position did pay its holder a welcome salary and allow him to travel about with a silver-plated rapier hanging from a leather baldric and to wear a black plumed hat with a silver band as his badge of office.

But by 1634 the bloom of infatuation which Kiliaen Van Rensselaer had felt for the tenants of de Laets burg showed signs of wilting. In April the patroon wrote Wouter Van Twiller, the director-general (governor) of New Netherlands, and displayed the beginnings of disappointment:

> *I see that Roeloff Janssen has grossly run up my account in drawing provisions, yes, practically the full allowance when there was stock. I think that his wife, mother, and sister and others must have given things away, which can not be allowed.*

Still, Jansen and the others were apparently good farmers; in spite of their cavalier treatment of his property, Van Rensselaer did not want to give them up easily. So, in the very same letter, he notes that the term of employment for which the three had been contracted in Amsterdam is just about over and, he continues,

> *...you might contract them for one year more. There will no doubt be some excuse for making them stay one year more, even if an increase had to be given them.*

Although these were obviously not the words of a man at the end of his patience, a new atmosphere of subservience to the will of the far-off patroon had come to Rensselaerwyck by 1634, an atmosphere which made it difficult for a man to strike out on his own unencumbered with responsibility to another. Roeliff Jansen saw that the time had come to move on once more, to cast off the ties which had held him and his family in place for the last four years, to leave no matter what riches Van Twiller might have to offer. So once his agreed term was up, Jansen packed up his family and cast about for a new home, without so much as a backward glance at the security and position that had been his at Fort Orange.

Strange as it may seem today, this yearning for open spaces found expression on a small island far to the south of Rensselaerwyck—Manhattan. Leaving Fort Orange for the last time in the late summer or early fall of 1634, Roeliff Jansen moved his family downriver to New Amsterdam and began working one of the Dutch West India Company's boweries (farms) there with the hope of eventually earning enough to strike out on his own. His mother-in-law, Tryn Roeloffs, contributed to the family's welfare by returning to an old occupation and becoming the company's official midwife, a job of more limited duties than it sounds since the population of the settlement in those days was still less than three hundred. Finally enough was accumulated by the family to allow Jansen to answer his dream and purchase a place of his own, and in 1636 he obtained a "groundbrief" or grant from Van Twiller for his chosen parcel—most of lower Manhattan, no less. On what was decidedly mediocre farming land, the new owner apparently planned to raise tobacco and perhaps some varieties of grain, but before he was able to do much beyond clearing the land, Roeliff Jansen died. Behind him he left a widow, Anneke, still in her early thirties, her moth-

er the midwife, four or perhaps five surviving children—
and the 62-acre farm.

With the death of her husband, Anneke Jans was
cast out alone into the rough social life of the tiny settlement with its population of homesick males. Apparently
she thrived. In 1638 she was wed again, this time to no
lowly farmer of indifferent means, but to the leader of the
Dutch Reformed Church in New Amsterdam and one of the
wealthiest men in the colony, Domine Everhard Bogardus.

A man of uneven temper, Bogardus soon found
himself hard-put defending his new wife's high spirited
ways. On one occasion, he verbally attacked none less than
Director Van Twiller at a wedding feast, giving his reason
(as the event was later reported) "that he had called your
wife a whore." The marriage must have been a difficult
one, the husband hot-blooded and the wife indiscriminately
passionate, but still it lasted. The properties of the two
were combined and Anneke bore several more children.
But Domine Bogardus was drowned in the fall of 1647
when the ship on which he was a passenger floundered off
the coast of England, and Anneke was made a widow once
more.

This time she returned to Fort Orange where she
quietly lived out her days in a small house on the corner of
the present State and James Streets, leaving her property in
New Amsterdam in the care of several of her children.
Following her death in 1663, this land was left in equal
shares to each of the offspring of both marriages who, not
wanting such an unproductive piece of property tied around
their necks, soon agreed to sell the Jansen farm to the
English governor of the time, Francis Lovelace.

But Lovelace was himself unable to maintain title
for he was deeply overextended financially and was soon
forced by circumstances and by his own incompetence to
transfer it as partial payment for a huge debt to the Duke of
York, the nominal protector of the colony. It remained in

his royal hands (he was later James II) only briefly, until 1704, when it was presented as a gift of the Crown to the parish of Trinity Church. So far so good, but as Manhattan real estate slowly began to assume increased value, the descendants of Anneke began to look with longing toward what they had so indiscriminately disposed of so many years before, and they began searching the transaction for loopholes. Finally, it was discovered that Cornelius, one of Bogardus' sons had, for some reason, not signed the original Bill of Sale. That was all that was needed, and in 1750 the heirs, now several generations removed from actual ownership, entered court to contest the distant exchange. The resulting litigation became, from its sheer length, the most famous in the history of New York real estate law, dragging on for more than 150 years before at last definitively decided in favor of Trinity Church in 1909. Although in the end the descendants got nothing for their troubles, the trial did assure for Roeliff Jansen a place in the history books — as a footnote at least.

So far, this brief history has not come anywhere near the Roeliff Jansen Kill, much less the Roe Jan area. The man never lived here, was never that important to the record of his times, so why has his name been plastered with such unconcern through the region? For the answer we must rely on a typical mixture of myth, legend, folklore, possible invention and on known historical fact, none of which is definitive in itself but whose sum is the closest we shall ever come.

First the history: the name of the creek dates from at least 1680 when it is mentioned as such in a petition from Robert Livingston I to Governor Edmond Andross requesting permission from the latter to negotiate with local Indians for the purchase of land along its banks. When the resulting transaction was committed to paper in July of 1683, the name comes up again and when the purchase was confirmed in November of the following year by Governor Dongan, there was reference to the name "Roeloff Johnson's Kill" as being then in "common" use. So the name goes back at least to 1680 and by inference, probably much farther. Still the question remains: why?

Next there is a legend which, although as unsubstantiated by documentation as most legends, offers an explanation which most historians who study the period are able to accept. According to this story, the post of *schepens* required some travel, at least as far as New Amsterdam, to report on conditions upriver and to receive instructions in return. Again, according to this version of events, Jansen embarked on one such trip in late winter or early spring of one year, probably 1633. He made his report to the authorities, received his orders and began his return voyage, probably in the company of settlers and supplies for Rensselaerwyck, since transport on the river was too dear to allow a boat to be at the exclusive disposal of a single minor official.

At that time of year travel on the Hudson was uncertain for the flimsy wooden krags and, while still fifty miles short of their goal, the ice closed in and held the little vessel fast. As the freeze grew harder, the passengers were able to walk to the nearby shore where they encountered first, a small and fortunately friendly encampment of Indians and second, the mouth of a fairly prominent stream, which until that time had somehow remained undiscovered and unnamed by passing traders and settlers moving upriver. The ice held the party in its grip for a full three weeks during which time they had frequent and altogether pleasant encounters with the Indians and made some tentative explorations of the land nearby. Finally, the boat was released and their long captivity came to an end. Before setting off on the voyage home, however, the members wished to memorialize their adventure somehow and since the stream by which they had been stranded for lo these many weeks was still virgin territory so far as Dutch cartographers were concerned, what better monument to their passage than a name for the creek? The name of one of their number perhaps? The government official? Roeliff Jansen?

So that, and until someone comes along with a better story, is how Roeliff Jansen Kill, and by extension the Roe Jan area got its name.

Reprinted from *A History of the Roeliff Jansen Area,* a publication of the Roeliff Jansen Historical Society, 1992.

A Note About the Contributors

Harold Faber, a former reporter and editor of the *New York Times* and now its Hudson Valley correspondent, lives in Ancram. He is the author of many books, the latest of which are *The Discoverers of America* and *From Sea to Sea: The Growth of the United States*.

Jeffrey E. Holmes, who lives in Great Barrington, Massachusetts, is the manager of the Kimberly-Clark Mill in Ancram.

Hilary Masters, a former resident of Ancramdale, is a well-known author. He is now the director of the creative writing program at the Carnegie-Mellon Institute in Pittsburgh. His latest book is a collection of short stories, *Success,* published in 1992.

Ethel Miller, a life-long resident of Ancram, lives on a farm that has been actively worked for more than 200 years. She is the historian of the Town of Ancram.

Sally Bottiggi Naramore, who lives in Kinderhook, wrote her history of the iron mill at Ancram for a symposium on the Livingstons, which was later published in the Bard College-Hudson Valley Studies book, *The Livingston Legacy.*

James Polk, who lived in Hillsdale, wrote his biography of Roeliff Jansen for the first book published by the Roeliff Jansen Historical Society, *A History of the Roeliff Jansen Area,* published in 1975.

Peter H. Stott, an industrial historian who lives in West Medford, Massachusetts, wrote his history of the mill in Ancram as part of a larger work, a history of industry in Columbia County, published by the Columbia County Historical Society.

Index

Following are the publications of the Roeliff Jansen Historical Society:

A History of the Roeliff Jansen Area, 1975.

Hello Central and Goodbye: Some Local Telephone Histories, 1976.

A History of the Roeliff Jansen Area, revised edition, 1990.

The Mill on the Roeliff Jansen Kill, 1993.

(For information or copies, write to the Roeliff Jansen Historical Society, Box 172, Copake Falls, New York 12517.)